268

The Blow-By-Blow Account Of Ali's Amazing Onslaught…

…And The Day The Records Tumbled

TREVOR JONES

Published by Sporting Declarations Books

www.sportingdeclarations.co.uk

PO Box 882, Sutton, Surrey, SM2 5AW

First published in 2002 by Sporting Declarations Books

ISBN 0 9535307 4 4

Cover Photographs

TOP:
Ali Brown in front of the AMP Oval scoreboard at the conclusion of an incredible match.
Photo by Phil Walter - Empics

BOTTOM:
Another crunching Ali Brown cover drive sends the ball speeding to the boundary.
Photo by Phil Walter - Empics

Typesetting and design by Trevor Jones

Printed and bound in Great Britain
by APG, Unit 9, Mitcham Industrial Estate, Streatham Road, Mitcham, CR4 2AP

Contents

1 INTRODUCTION
AN INCREDIBLE DAY OF DRAMA AND HISTORY

I've been fortunate enough to witness almost every game played by the Surrey County Cricket Club first team over the past five years and I have seen some phenomenal cricket in that time - superlative strokeplay, skilful swing and seam bowling, blinding catches, mesmerising spin bowling and many memorable matches, including some almost unbelievable comebacks from adversity. Most of the truly astounding performances have come, as you would expect, in the four-day arena where Surrey have proved to be so dominant in recent times. Even though the club has had many hugely talented players at its disposal, the limited-overs form of the game has never really been Surrey's forte, despite the fact that the past seven seasons have brought two Benson & Hedges Cup triumphs and two Sunday/National League trophies. There have, however, been some terrific matches and individual performances in that period... but nothing to compare with what took place on Wednesday 19th June 2002.

The spectators who were present at The AMP Oval that day can consider themselves very lucky indeed, for they witnessed one of the most incredible one-day matches ever played. Even though conditions were as close as possible to being perfect for batting, no one could have guessed what was about to happen as Ian Ward and Ali Brown took guard on a beautiful morning in London SE11.

The weather had been totally different in Edinburgh three weeks earlier when Surrey had started their 2002 Cheltenham & Gloucester Trophy campaign with a third-round game against Scotland. At a very wet Grange Cricket Club ground, a first-day washout was followed by a reserve-day Duckworth-Lewis victory for Surrey by 55 runs in conditions that were far from ideal. Although I have, personally, enjoyed the two recent trips north of the border, it would seem that the Scottish air isn't much to Alistair Brown's liking - having made a third-ball duck when Surrey met Scotland at the same ground in the UK's premier cup competition back in 1999, he fared even worse on this occasion, drilling a catch to cover from the first delivery of the match.

Things were to be very different in the next round!

Trevor Jones

2 ALL ABOUT BROWNY

For those people reading this booklet who are not particularly familiar with the man and his career, this section gives you a full rundown of basic facts and figures relevant to Alistair Brown's career with Surrey and England.

One of the most entertaining and aggressive batsmen to ever play the game of cricket, 'Browny' has never compromised his positive approach to batting since first appearing on the county scene in 1990. As the facts below reveal, he made an amazing impact early in his career by scoring three quick-fire centuries in his first season of County Championship cricket and unlike most batsmen, who tend to play more conservatively as they get older, he has retained the same forthright style and approach as he has moved into his thirties. That's not to say he can't play a highly disciplined and measured innings when the need arises, however, for we have seen many fine examples of this in recent times.

Boasting a first-class average in excess of 43 runs per innings and a priceless ability to convert a very high proportion of his fifties into hundreds and many of his hundreds into big hundreds, it remains a mystery as to why Ali has never been given a chance to play for England at Test level. Sixteen one-day international caps offer some consolation but, even in that form of the game, there is a feeling that he wasn't utilised as well as he might have been. Many good judges have expressed the view that he should have been given more opportunities to display and adapt his special talent in the international arena during an extended and unbroken run in the side but, sadly, there was less continuity in the selection of the England side in those days. England's loss has been his county's gain, however, and there is no doubt that Alistair Brown will go down in history as one of Surrey's all-time greats.

ALISTAIR DUNCAN BROWN
Right-handed batsman
Occasional off-break bowler and wicket-keeper
5' 10"
Born February 11, 1970 in Beckenham, Kent

Career Milestones And Highlights

1990
* Engaged by Surrey
* Makes first-team limited-overs debut in the Sunday League versus Somerset at Weston-super-Mare, 5th August, scoring 32 in a Surrey win by six wickets.

1991

* Benson & Hedges Cup debut against Warwickshire at The Oval, 7th May, scoring 37 as Surrey lose by one run.

1992

* Makes his first-class debut versus Derbyshire at The Oval, 2nd to 4th June, scoring 6 and 0 in a drawn match.
* Scores three first-class centuries during the season, including his maiden ton, 111 versus Nottinghamshire at The Oval in only his third match. Follows up with 175 against Durham at Durham in his fourth game and 129 versus Somerset on his ninth appearance. All three hundreds rank among the eight fastest of the season, coming from 79, 71 and 78 balls respectively.
* Records maiden limited-overs century for Surrey in the Sunday League - 113 against Glamorgan at Llanelli.

1993

* Premier Cup competition debut against Dorset at The Oval in the Nat West Trophy, 22nd June, but doesn't bat as Surrey win by ten wickets.
* Represents England for the first time in the World Six-A-Side competition in Singapore (played again in 1994, 1995 and 1997)

1994

* Awarded county cap by Surrey

1995

* Raises his career-best first-class score to 187 with a match-winning innings against Gloucestershire at The Oval in the first game of the season as Surrey come from behind to win after following-on.

1996

* Makes one-day international debut for England in the first game of the series versus India at The Oval, 23rd to 24th May, scoring 37 in a rain-ruined no-result match.
* Scores 118 in the third one-day international at Old Trafford and wins the Man Of The Match award.
* Totals 471 runs at an average of 33.64 as Surrey win the Sunday League title, the Club's first trophy for fourteen years.

1997

* Scores 203, off 119 balls, against Hampshire in the Sunday League - the first-ever (and still the only) double-century recorded in the competition.
* His 256 runs (average 32.00) help Surrey on their way to Benson & Hedges Cup glory at Lord's.

1997/98
* Represents England in the Champions Trophy in Sharjah - England win the competition under the captaincy of Adam Hollioake.

1998
* Scores a 72-ball century against Northamptonshire at The Oval to become joint winner, with Carl Hooper, of the EDS Walter Lawrence Trophy for the fastest first-class hundred of the season.
* Plays twice for England in the Texaco Trophy series versus South Africa, scoring a 31-ball half-century in the match at Headingley to set a new mark for the fastest fifty in the history of the competition. Also plays in three matches in the Emirates Triangular Tournament against South Africa and Sri Lanka.

1998/99
* Represents England in the Wills International Cup in Bangladesh.

1999
* Records a new career-best score of 265 against Middlesex at Lord's.
* Heads the batting averages by scoring 1127 runs at 51.22 as Surrey claim their first County Championship crown since 1971.

2000
* Hits a career-best unbeaten 295 versus Leicestershire at Oakham School.
* Tops the county batting averages with 935 runs at 51.94 as Surrey retain their County Championship title. Also accumulates 330 runs (average 23.57) to help the team win Division Two of the National League.

2001
* Represents England again in the one-day Nat West series against Australia and Pakistan.
* Contributes 219 runs at an average of 43.80 as Surrey win the Benson & Hedges Cup.

2002
* Enjoys a well-deserved benefit season, scoring 1211 runs (average 50.45), including five centuries, as Surrey win their third County Championship title in four years.
* Smashes the world record for the highest individual score made in a limited-overs match when he records a phenomenal 268 against Glamorgan in the fourth round of the Cheltenham & Gloucester Trophy at The AMP Oval. A whole host of records tumble as he becomes the first man to score two first-class limited-overs double-centuries.

Career Bests

Highest Score
One-Day Internationals - 118 v India at Old Trafford, 1996
First-Class Cricket - 295 not out v Leicestershire at Oakham School, 2000
County Championship - 295 not out v Leicestershire at Oakham School, 2000
Premier Limited-Overs Cup Competition - 268 v Glamorgan at The AMP Oval, 2002
Benson & Hedges Cup - 117 not out v Sussex at Hove, 1996
Sunday League/National League - 203 v Hampshire at Guildford, 1996

Best Bowling
First-Class Cricket - 1 for 56 v Lancashire at Old Trafford, 2000
County Championship - 1 for 56 v Lancashire at Old Trafford, 2000
Sunday League/National League - 3 for 39 v Nottinghamshire at Trent Bridge, 2000

Career Batting Aggregates/Statistics

First-Class double-centuries - 2
First-Class centuries - 32
First-Class half-centuries - 39
First-Class catches - 177
First-Class stumpings - 1
1000 First-Class Runs In A Season - 6 times (1993-95, 1998-99, 2002)
Most First-Class Runs In A Season - 1382 in 1993
Has scored a first-class century against every other county except Lancashire

Limited-Overs double-centuries - 2
Limited-Overs centuries - 15
Limited-Overs half-centuries - 32
Limited-Overs catches - 83
Benson & Hedges Cup Man Of The Match 'Gold Awards' - 4
Premier Cup Competition Man Of The Match awards - 1

PLEASE NOTE - For the purposes of this book, the Gillette Cup, the Nat West Trophy and the Cheltenham & Gloucester Trophy are referred to as 'the premier cup competition'. Gillette sponsored the competition from 1963 to 1980 inclusive, Nat West from 1981 to 2000 inclusive and Cheltenham & Gloucester from 2001 to the current day. Matches were 65 overs per side in 1963, 60 per side from 1964-1998 inclusive and 50 per side since 1999.

ONE-DAY INTERNATIONAL APPEARANCES (1996 to 2001)

Season	Opponents	Venue	Runs Scored	Balls Faced	Catches Taken
1996	India	Oval	37	52	-
1996	India	Headingley	0	2	1
1996	India	Old Trafford	118	137	-
1997/98	India	Sharjah	18	25	-
1997/98	West Indies	Sharjah	10	18	-
1997/98	Pakistan	Sharjah	41	47	-
1997/98	West Indies	Sharjah	1	13	1
1998	South Africa	Old Trafford	13	15	-
1998	South Africa	Headingley	59	40	-
1998	Sri Lanka	Lord's	12	11	1
1998	South Africa	Edgbaston	0	3	-
1998	Sri Lanka	Lord's	18	18	1
1998/99	South Africa	Dhaka	6	10	2
2001	Pakistan	Edgbaston	8	13	-
2001	Australia	Bristol	12	16	-
2001	Australia	Oval	1	7	-

ONE-DAY INTERNATIONAL BATTING RECORD

Matches	I	NO	Runs	HS	Ave	100s	50s	Runs/100 balls	Ct
16	16	0	354	118	22.13	1	1	82.90	6

ONE-DAY INTERNATIONAL BOWLING RECORD

Matches	O	M	R	W	Ave	5WI	3WI	Strike Rate	Econ
16	1	0	5	0	-	-	-	-	5.00

FIRST-CLASS BATTING RECORD (all first-class matches)

Year	M	I	NO	Runs	HS	Average	100s	50s	Ct	St
1992	11	16	1	740	175	49.33	3	3	6	-
1993	19	34	3	1382	150*	44.58	3	4	18	-
1994	17	24	2	1049	172	47.68	2	6	16	-
1995	16	29	4	1054	187	42.16	3	3	20	-
1996	15	24	2	462	69	21.00	-	4	18	-
1997	14	21	1	848	170*	42.40	3	2	11	-
1998	15	22	1	1036	155	49.33	4	6	20	-
1999	17	26	4	1127	265	51.22	4	2	31	1
2000	16	23	5	935	295*	51.94	2	4	16	-
2001	13	20	-	630	122	31.50	3	2	3	-
2002	16	26	2	1211	188	50.45	5	3	18	-
Totals	169	265	25	10474	295*	43.64	32	39	177	1

FIRST-CLASS BOWLING RECORD (all first-class matches)

Year	O	M	R	W	Average	5WI	BB	Strike Rate
1992	16	1	78	0	-	-	-	-
1993	1	0	6	0	-	-	-	-
1994	15	1	47	0	-	-	-	-
1995	-	-	-	-	-	-	-	-
1996	6	2	8	0	-	-	-	-
1997	16	4	37	0	-	-	-	-
1998	2	1	2	0	-	-	-	-
1999	26	3	80	0	-	-	-	-
2000	28	9	70	1	70.00	-	1/56	168.0
2001	23	1	97	0	-	-	-	-
2002	3	0	7	0	-	-	-	-
Totals	136	22	432	1	432.00	-	1/56	798.0

LIMITED-OVERS BATTING RECORD
(Sunday/National Lge, Nat West/C&G Trophy, B&H Cup only)

Year	M	I	NO	Runs	HS	Average	100	50	Ct	St
1990	4	4	-	114	56	28.50	-	1	4	-
1991	8	7	-	170	45	24.29	-	-	-	-
1992	24	24	3	755	113	35.95	2	2	4	-
1993	21	18	1	449	103	26.41	1	3	7	-
1994	25	23	3	871	142	43.55	2	4	4	-
1995	22	21	1	604	100	30.20	1	2	8	-
1996	24	24	2	943	117	42.86	1	6	5	-
1997	24	24	1	877	203	38.13	2	4	6	-
1998	25	24	-	494	74	20.54	-	1	7	-
1999	20	20	1	488	105	25.68	1	-	9	-
2000	21	21	-	427	59	20.33	-	2	11	-
2001	22	20	2	787	130	43.72	4	1	9	-
2002	24	24	-	899	268	37.46	1	6	9	-
Totals	264	254	14	7878	268	32.83	15	32	83	-

LIMITED-OVERS BOWLING RECORD
(Sunday/National Lge, Nat West/C&G Trophy, B&H Cup only)

Year	O	M	R	W	Average	4wI	BB	Econ
1999	25.5	0	141	3	47.00	-	1/20	5.46
2000	12	0	66	4	16.50	-	3/39	5.50
2001	8	0	54	1	54.00	-	1/40	6.75
Totals	45.5	0	261	8	32.63	-	3/39	5.69

3 THE STORY OF THE MATCH

THE TEAMS AND THE TOSS

Surrey go into the match without Graham Thorpe, Alex Tudor and Mark Butcher, who are rested after their efforts in the recently-completed third Test against Sri Lanka. Saqlain Mushtaq is preferred to Ian Salisbury as Surrey's sole spinner and Alec Stewart plays purely as a batsman to protect a minor hand injury - Jon Batty keeps wicket. Glamorgan captain Steve James misses out as his young daughter is ill so David Hemp takes his place in the batting line-up and Robert Croft stands in as skipper. With Alex Wharf injured, Andrew Davies gets the nod ahead of the speedy but less reliable Simon Jones.

On a bright sunny morning with conditions looking perfect for batting Adam Hollioake has no hesitation in electing to bat upon winning the toss. Today's pitch is set well over to the eastern side of the ground, about three strips from the edge of the square, leaving a fairly short boundary of some 50-60 yards down towards the gasholders.

1ST OVER - MICHAEL KASPROWICZ 1
VAUXHALL END

Ian Ward opens Surrey's account by pushing a single to midwicket from the fifth delivery while Ali Brown is off the mark next ball with a run to third man.

2-0 Ali Brown 1, Ian Ward 1   *Kasprowicz 1-0-2-0*

2ND OVER - ANDREW DAVIES 1
PAVILION END

Brown fails to make proper contact with a pull stroke from the second ball but still picks up two runs to fine leg. Other than a leg-side wide, it's a very quiet over.

5-0 Ali Brown 3, Ian Ward 1   *Davies 1-0-3-0*

3RD OVER - MICHAEL KASPROWICZ 2
VAUXHALL END

There's no sign of what is to come as Ian Ward faces the whole of an accurate over, profiting only from an off-driven two from the second ball.

7-0 Ali Brown 3, Ian Ward 3   *Kasprowicz 2-0-4-0*

4TH OVER - ANDREW DAVIES 2
PAVILION END

Ali Brown sparks into life, taking 4, 2, 4 from the first three balls of the over with drives through extra cover and backward point and a pull wide of mid-on. He slices the fifth ball of the over to third man for a single.

18-0 Ali Brown 14, Ian Ward 3   *Davies 2-0-14-0*

5TH OVER - MICHAEL KASPROWICZ 3
VAUXHALL END

Kasprowicz keeps Brown quiet for the first five balls before the Surrey opener blasts the final delivery over cover for a boundary.

22-0 Ali Brown 18, Ian Ward 3   *Kasprowicz 3-0-8-0*

6TH OVER - ANDREW DAVIES 3
PAVILION END

Ian Ward's fortunate bottom edge past the keeper earns him three runs from the second ball of a tidy over.

25-0 Ali Brown 18, Ian Ward 6   *Davies 3-0-17-0*

7TH OVER - MICHAEL KASPROWICZ 4
VAUXHALL END

The over starts sedately, yielding just a leg-bye and a leg-glanced single for Brown, before Ward picks up boundaries from the final two balls with a clip backward of square leg and a cover drive.

35-0 Ali Brown 19, Ian Ward 14   ***Kasprowicz 4-0-17-0***

8TH OVER - ANDREW DAVIES 4
PAVILION END

Brown starts the over with two authentic fours, lofted over extra cover and driven along the ground through cover point, but ends with a more fortunate boundary, squeezing a full-length delivery all along the ground past the wicketkeeper.

47-0 Ali Brown 31, Ian Ward 14   ***Davies 4-0-29-0***

TJ - How did you feel you were playing at this early stage?

AB - I'd been in good form for quite a while, though I was a little disappointed to have scored a few good fifties without turning them into hundreds - for example, I made fifty off about 30 balls at Northampton in the Norwich Union League but didn't go on from there. But I felt my weight, my balance and my feet were all in good shape so I thought a big score might be around the corner… I didn't know it was going to be as big as it turned out to be though! The ball swung around for the first few overs but then Wardy and I hit a couple of boundaries and things became a bit easier from there.

9TH OVER - MICHAEL KASPROWICZ 5
VAUXHALL END

Following a single to Ward and a leg-bye, the left-handed Surrey opener brings up his side's fifty with a clip to midwicket for two from the final ball of the over.
MILESTONE
50 up/50 partnership in 9.0 overs.

51-0 Ali Brown 31, Ian Ward 17   ***Kasprowicz 5-0-20-0***

10TH OVER - DARREN THOMAS 1
PAVILION END

Darren Thomas replaces Andrew Davies and Brown promptly blasts 6, 4, 6 from the Glamorgan seamer's second, third and fourth balls - a pull over the midwicket boundary is followed by a lofted extra cover drive and a drive over wide mid-on for another maximum. Brown and Surrey are now really flying.

67-0 Ali Brown 47, Ian Ward 17   ***Thomas 1-0-16-0***

TJ - Was that a deliberate attempt to unsettle the new bowler?

AB - Not really. Occasionally you might target someone but on this occasion it was just a very good pitch with very true bounce and his length was variable.

11TH OVER - MICHAEL KASPROWICZ 6
VAUXHALL END

Another good over from Glamorgan's Australian import, yielding only four runs via a thick inside edge to the backward square leg boundary by Ward from the fourth ball.

71-0 Ali Brown 47, Ian Ward 21   ***Kasprowicz 6-0-24-0***

12TH OVER - DARREN THOMAS 2
PAVILION END

Glamorgan's stand-in captain, Robert Croft, keeps faith with Thomas despite the 16-run mauling of his opening over... and that faith is almost repaid as Brown edges the first delivery high to the right of Mark Wallace behind the wicket. The young wicketkeeper gets both hands to the ball but he is unable to hold on to a hot chance and two runs result as the ball ricochets away towards fine third man. Missing a catch offered by a batsman as dangerous as Ali Brown can often be costly, a fact that is underlined as he slices the next delivery, a full toss, to third man for the single that brings up his fifty. Thomas is probably already thinking that it's not going to be his day as Ward then gains two runs from an inside edge past the keeper two balls later. An eventful over is completed by a leg-side wide and a single whipped through midwicket by the Surrey left-hander.

MILESTONE

Ali Brown's half-century came from 38 balls and included 2 sixes and 7 fours.

78-0 Ali Brown 50, Ian Ward 24   *Thomas 2-0-23-0*

TJ - It wasn't an easy chance for Wallace but did you think it was one that he should really have held?

AB - It was a hard slash so the ball was really travelling but I'm not sure how wide it was - it wasn't a straightforward chance. Sometimes you have a bit of luck, though, as I did here.

13TH OVER - ANDREW DAVIES 5
VAUXHALL END

After a good opening spell, Kasprowicz gives way to Andrew Davies, who has thereby switched ends. He gets off to a bad start as Ward drives his opening delivery through the covers for four, before a thick edge to third man puts Brown back on strike. The right-hander follows his fellow opener's example by crashing his first ball of the over to the cover fence. A single, driven wide of mid-on, and two leg-byes complete a rather shabby over.

90-0 Ali Brown 55, Ian Ward 29   *Davies 5-0-39-0*

14TH OVER - DARREN THOMAS 3
PAVILION END

Thomas is still unable to locate a consistent line or length as Brown drives him over the rope at square cover for six and picks off a single with a square drive before Ward cuts the fifth delivery to the point boundary to bring up the Surrey hundred.

MILESTONE

100 up/100 partnership in 13.5 overs. The second fifty of the innings came up in just 29 balls.

101-0 Ali Brown 62, Ian Ward 33   *Thomas 3-0-34-0*

15TH OVER - ROBERT CROFT 1
VAUXHALL END

With his seamers unable to stem the flow of runs, Robert Croft brings himself on to bowl the fifteenth over. It's a bold move, with the fielding restrictions still at their most severe, and it doesn't really pay off - after a single apiece to the openers from the first two balls, Brown advances to the third ball and lofts it back down the ground for six. Croft's opening-over blues are amplified when the same batsman thick-edges a cut at the final delivery and picks up four runs to the third man boundary.

CAREER BEST

Perhaps surprisingly, when he reached 73 Ali Brown posted a new personal highest score in the premier cup competition, beating the 72 he scored against Holland at The Oval in 1996.

113-0 Ali Brown 73, Ian Ward 34   *Croft 1-0-12-0*

TJ - I assume it represents something of a moral victory if you are able to force a spinner into the attack within the first fifteen overs?

AB - It depends on the situation. We'd played well up to here and with the wicket so good it was easy to work the bowlers around. We'd got off to a good start so we just looked to carry on playing in the same vein. Sometimes you might think 'there's no man out there so I might target that area' but at that point we were scoring sufficiently quickly that there was no need to take any risks.

TJ - Having had a chance to assess the pitch and the bowling what sort of total did you feel would be par for the course at this stage?

AB - We didn't have a particular total in mind, we just wanted to keep on playing as we were - the runs kept flowing and there were no really quiet overs.

TJ - I was amazed when I discovered that your previous best score in the competition was only 72. Do you have any idea why this competition hadn't been particularly successful for you until this match?

AB - There might be a number of reasons. In the opening round you play a minor county so sometimes you don't get in if you are batting at five. It also depends on how far you get in the competition and the C&G hasn't been a particularly great competition for us, so that also limits opportunities. I've often felt that we used to just bat normally at the top of the order, meaning that numbers four to seven would then end up coming in just to give it a bash. But I was more than aware that my best score was 72 against Holland and I was a little bit embarrassed by that because I've always said that I wanted to score a double-century in every competition. Having a best score that was against the equivalent of a minor county was obviously nothing to write home about, so I was very keen to get past that landmark.

16TH OVER - ADRIAN DALE 1
PAVILION END

A shell-shocked Darren Thomas is withdrawn from the firing line and replaced by the medium-paced Dale. It proves to be a good change - after Ward picks up a single from the first ball, Brown profits only to the tune of a brace of twos, clipped to deep midwicket and cut through point.

118-0 Ali Brown 77, Ian Ward 35   *Dale 1-0-5-0*

14

17TH OVER - ROBERT CROFT 2
VAUXHALL END

Croft comes up with the most economical over since the sixth over of the day as only three runs - two singles to Ward and one to Brown - accrue.

121-0 Ali Brown 78, Ian Ward 37   *Croft 2-0-15-0*

18TH OVER - ADRIAN DALE 2
PAVILION END

A five-run over appears to be acceptable to the visitors, giving them just a modicum of control after the early carnage. Ward has a lucky moment when he edges the fifth ball past his leg stump for a single but Brown continues to accumulate runs steadily, picking up one run for a forcing stroke to deep mid-off and two for a leg glance. The extras count has risen to seven following a leg-bye from the first delivery.

126-0 Ali Brown 81, Ian Ward 38   *Dale 2-0-9-0*

19TH OVER - ROBERT CROFT 3
VAUXHALL END

Another tidy three-run over - two singles to Ward and one to Brown - gives Glamorgan a little more respite.

129-0 Ali Brown 82, Ian Ward 40   *Croft 3-0-18-0*

20TH OVER - ADRIAN DALE 3
PAVILION END

A carbon copy of the previous over from Croft - Ward picking up two singles to Brown's one - sees the Welshmen recovering a little more ground.

132-0 Ali Brown 83, Ian Ward 42   *Dale 3-0-12-0*

21ST OVER - ROBERT CROFT 4
VAUXHALL END

Surrey are up and running again as Ward slog-sweeps the off-spinner's second delivery out of the ground for six. The last four balls of the over all bring singles to deep-set fielders, with Ward completing his half-century from the fifth ball.
MILESTONE
Ian Ward's fifty arrived from 61balls and included 1 six and 5 fours.

142-0 Ali Brown 85, Ian Ward 50   *Croft 4-0-28-0*

22ND OVER - ADRIAN DALE 4
PAVILION END

Dale is accurate enough but is still easily milked for six runs - a two and two singles to Brown, two singles to Ward.

148-0 Ali Brown 89, Ian Ward 52   *Dale 4-0-18-0*

23RD OVER - DEAN COSKER 1
VAUXHALL END

Off-spin gives way to left-arm spin as Dean Cosker enters the fray, replacing his skipper at the Vauxhall end. It makes little difference to Ian Ward, however, as he slog-sweeps the third ball of the over into the road outside the ground again. Four singles - two to each batsman - also accrue in a ten-run over which has seen the Surrey total pass 150.

150 up/150 partnership in 22.2 overs. The third fifty of the innings took a comparatively pedestrian 51balls.

158-0 Ali Brown 91, Ian Ward 60   *Cosker 1-0-10-0*

24TH OVER - ADRIAN DALE 5
PAVILION END

After an eight-over break, Brown is back on the boundary trail, driving the second ball of the over through extra cover for four. He follows up with a cut backward of square for two and a forcing stroke to deep cover for a single. Ward then makes it an excellent over for Surrey by edging and square-driving boundaries from the final two deliveries of the over. Dale has thus conceded almost as many runs (fifteen) in this over as he had done in his first four.

CLUB RECORD

When the score reached 165, Ali Brown and Ian Ward set a new record for the highest opening partnership for Surrey in the premier cup competition, beating the unbroken stand of 164 compiled by Darren Bicknell and Alec Stewart against Dorset at The Oval in 1993.

173-0 Ali Brown 98, Ian Ward 68   *Dale 5-0-33-0*

25TH OVER - DEAN COSKER 2
VAUXHALL END

Having driven the third ball of the over down to long-on for a single and then watched his partner clip the next delivery to midwicket for another run, Brown completes a magnificent century with a push into the covers for a single. A leg-side wide has pushed the extras tally up to eight during the over. Surrey reach the halfway point of their innings with a very satisfactory 177 runs on the board.

MILESTONE

Ali Brown's first century in this competition, and sixteenth in all competitive limited-overs cricket, came from just 80 balls and included 4 sixes and 10 fours

177-0 Ali Brown 100, Ian Ward 69   *Cosker 2-0-14-0*

26TH OVER - DARREN THOMAS 4
PAVILION END

Thomas returns to the attack and starts with a leg-side wide. Each batsman then picks off a single to long-off before Brown rips into the Glamorgan seamer again, driving the fourth delivery of the over through extra cover for four, pulling the next out of the ground over midwicket and pushing the last ball to square cover for a single. Fourteen runs have therefore come from the over.

CLUB RECORD

When the partnership reached 184 it became the highest for any wicket for Surrey in the history of the premier cup competition, beating 180 (for the third wicket) by Graham Thorpe and David Ward against Lancashire at the Oval in 1994

191-0 Ali Brown 112, Ian Ward 70   *Thomas 4-0-48-0*

TJ - Having already handed out some very rough treatment to Darren Thomas, were you surprised to see him return to the attack so quickly?

AB - I wasn't particularly surprised because he can be quite an impressive bowler

at times. He's got a bit of pace about him and he was perhaps being used more as a strike bowler, looking to get a breakthrough, but he tended to bowl too short and most balls of that length were put away to the boundary.

27TH OVER - DEAN COSKER 3
VAUXHALL END

Having been put on strike by a single to mid-on by Brown from the first ball, Ward continues the six-hitting spree by advancing on Cosker and driving him into the road over wide long-on. Glamorgan's left-arm spinner keeps a tight rein for the rest of the over, however, allowing just a single to each batsman.

MILESTONE

200 up/200 partnership in 27.0 overs. The fourth fifty of the innings was the fastest so far, coming up in just 28 deliveries.

200-0 Ali Brown 114, Ian Ward 77   *Cosker 3-0-23-0*

28TH OVER - DARREN THOMAS 5
PAVILION END

Just when Thomas, and his captain, were thinking that things couldn't get any worse they do... an astonishingly poor over costs twenty-two runs. The first half of the over yields a single to each batsman, a leg-side wide and another wayward leg-side delivery which evades the diving Wallace and runs to the boundary, counting as five wides. Brown then rubs salt into the wounds, taking 4, 6, 4 from the last three balls with a slice over point, a pull out of the ground at backward square leg and a lofted extra cover drive. Surrey are now well set for a huge total and Thomas' figures make gruesome reading.

CLUB RECORD

When the score reached 222, Ali Brown and Ian Ward created a new record for the highest partnership for any wicket for Surrey in all limited-overs cricket, overhauling the 218-run stand compiled by Alan Butcher and Geoff Howarth in a Sunday League match against Gloucestershire at The Oval in 1976.

222-0 Ali Brown 129, Ian Ward 78   *Thomas 5-0-70-0*

29TH OVER - MICHAEL KASPROWICZ 7
VAUXHALL END

With his problems increasing by the over, Croft makes the very sensible move of bringing back his main strike bowler in an attempt to secure a much-needed breakthrough. Ironically, the big Australian starts with two leg-side wides, though the rest of the over is pretty respectable, two off-driven singles and a square-driven two coming Ward's way and Brown managing just a single from the two balls that he faces.

CAREER BEST

Ian Ward's best score in the premier cup competition was registered when he reached 82. His previous highest score was 81 against Yorkshire at Headingley in 2001.

229-0 Ali Brown 130, Ian Ward 82   *Kasprowicz 7-0-31-0*

17

30TH OVER - ADRIAN DALE 6
PAVILION END

The return of Dale at the Pavilion end makes it a double bowling change, though his return is not as successful as Kasprowicz's. After Ward scurries through for a short single from the first ball, Brown cuts the next delivery to the rope at point, lofts the fourth over wide long-off for four and cuts the final ball to the sweeper at deep cover for a single. Ten runs in total. It is reckoned that in 50-over cricket an end-of-innings total can be quite accurately estimated by doubling the score after thirty overs, assuming there are plenty of wickets in hand. By this reckoning, Surrey's final score today should be 478... even in this situation, that seems highly unlikely!

239-0 Ali Brown 139, Ian Ward 83   *Dale 6-0-43-0*

TJ - Did you now have any personal target or prospective team total in mind? Did the rule about doubling the score after thirty overs to get an idea of the final total cross your mind?

AB - I've never heard of that thirty-over formula before and I'm not sure how accurate it could be because we've found over the last few years that as the ball gets older it tends to go soft and reverse-swing, making it increasingly difficult to get the ball away. We don't really look to set a target like that anyway - we just look to be positive early on and try to build to as big a total as possible from there.

31ST OVER - MICHAEL KASPROWICZ 8
VAUXHALL END

Although Kasprowicz is again unable to remove either of the Surrey openers, he concedes just five runs - a steer backward of point for four and a square drive for one by Brown - from an accurate over.

244-0 Ali Brown 144, Ian Ward 83   *Kasprowicz 8-0-36-0*

32ND OVER - ROBERT CROFT 5
PAVILION END

After just one over, Dale gives way to Croft at the pavilion end. The former England off-spinner and stand-in captain doesn't enjoy his return, though, as Brown pull-drives his second ball for six, sweeps the next for four and drives the sixth to long-on for a single in an eleven-run over which brings several milestones and records.

MILESTONES
The six took Brown to a magnificent 150 from 104 balls with 7 sixes and 16 fours. The four brought up the Surrey 250 and the 250 partnership in 31.3 overs. The fifth fifty of the innings therefore arrived in a mere 27 deliveries, making it the fastest fifty of the innings so far.

CLUB RECORD
When Brown reached 150 he claimed the record for the highest score by a Surrey player in the history of the premier cup competition, beating Grahame Clinton's 146 against Kent at Canterbury in 1985.

255-0 Ali Brown 155, Ian Ward 83   *Croft 5-0-39-0*

33RD OVER - MICHAEL KASPROWICZ 9
VAUXHALL END

Croft's desperate need for a wicket forces him to keep Kasprowicz going, a decision he ends up regretting as Ward drives the Australian's third delivery to the extra cover rope and Brown lofts the final ball over mid-off for another boundary. With each batsman also picking up a single, the over costs ten.

265-0 Ali Brown 160, Ian Ward 88   *Kasprowicz 9-0-46-0*

34TH OVER - ROBERT CROFT 6
PAVILION END

Ward's clip to midwicket for a single is followed by another lost ball as Brown slog-sweeps the third ball for six. Croft's improved control allows only three off-driven singles from the remainder of the over, but the damage is already done.

275-0 Ali Brown 168, Ian Ward 90   *Croft 6-0-49-0*

35TH OVER - DEAN COSKER 4
VAUXHALL END

Keeping an over of Kasprowicz in hand, the Glamorgan captain turns again to his spin partner, Dean Cosker. Following a leg-side wide, Brown clips to midwicket for two and on-drives for a single before Ward swings the fourth ball high over midwicket for six and drives the next along the ground to deep midwicket for a single. An eleven-run over represents a far-from-ideal return for Cosker.

CAREER BEST

Ian Ward's career-best limited-overs score arrived when he reached 96. His previous best was 91 v Middlesex in the Sunday League at Guildford in 1998.

286-0 Ali Brown 171, Ian Ward 97   *Cosker 4-0-34-0*

36TH OVER - ROBERT CROFT 7
PAVILION END

There's joy for Glamorgan at last as the first delivery of the thirty-sixth over sees Ian Ward dismissed, the ball somehow making its way onto the stumps, possibly via his pads, as he shuffles across his wicket. It's a great pity that he has fallen just three runs short of a well-deserved ton but at least he has the consolation of having taken part in a record-breaking partnership which has put his team on the way to a huge total. The 286-run stand ranks as the fourth-highest opening partnership in first-class limited-overs cricket, falling forty short of the 326 posted by Ghulam Ali and Sohail Jaffar for PIA against ADBP in 2000/01. In UK terms, it rates second behind the 311 recorded by Tony Wright and Nick Trainor for Gloucestershire against Scotland at Bristol in the 1997 Nat West Trophy. Having waited patiently for his turn to bat, Mark Ramprakash is quickly under way with a brace of singles to long-on, while Brown increases his score by one with a drive to deep midwicket.

289-1 Ali Brown 172, Mark Ramprakash 2   *Croft 7-0-52-1*

TJ - Although Wardy's knock was clearly overshadowed by yours, it was in fact a terrific innings, wasn't it?

AB - Yes, he played exceptionally well and I didn't feel that either of us was going to get out. When it did come, the dismissal was a little bit freakish, too, as he was bowled via his thigh pad.

TJ - And 286 for the first wicket was rather a good start!

AB - Yes, it was a good partnership. I think both Wardy and I were a little disappointed that we batted so low down the order in the Benson & Hedges matches at the start of the season. I was usually at five and he was six but we changed things around after the B&H debacle and I think we proved in this match that we make a very good opening partnership in one-day cricket. We run well, we're a left-hand/right-hand combination and he's played very positively and exceptionally well this year.

TJ - How much does it help to open with a left-hander, like Wardy, rather than a right-hander?

AB - I think it's good if you can find a right-hand/left-hand pairing because it does make the bowlers adjust their line a little bit. It doesn't always work, of course, but I think we are a good combination because we complement each other nicely and, because we run well together, we can rotate the strike regularly. I'd like to think our one-day partnership could be maintained for some time.

TJ - Judging by what you've said, you feel you should always open for Surrey in one-day cricket.

AB - I've said for quite a while now that I think I should open because even if I get out early - if the ball is, say, swinging or seaming around a lot - we can just revert to batting the way we normally do in the Championship. I do think that in one-day cricket you have to take chances - it's a game of chance - and you've got to be fearless. One game this season that stands out for me was the one against Hampshire in the Benson & Hedges, where I was stuck in the dressing room waiting to bat, getting totally frustrated, just watching as the required run rate went up and up. I eventually went in with the rate at seven or eight an over and I was thinking that we never should have got into that situation. If I had opened then I'm sure we would never have reached that position and, even if I had got out early, then at least we would have given it a try.

*TJ - Is there **never** any situation where you feel you should bat in the middle-order then?*

AB - I like opening because the ball is hard early on, the fielders are up and it gives me a chance to play positively at that time of the innings. Having said that, I think there might be rare occasions when we could revert to an orthodox line-up with me at five. One of those was the C&G semi-final at Headingley this year when we lost the toss and got put in on a wicket that had been cut about five minutes before the start of play. In the end, though, I think we felt that we'd batted so well in the competition up to that point that we'd stick with the same batting order.

37TH OVER - DEAN COSKER 5
VAUXHALL END

Cosker keeps thing pretty quiet, conceding just four singles. He does, however, slightly spoil an otherwise good over with a pair of leg-side wides.

295-1 Ali Brown 174, Mark Ramprakash 4   **Cosker 5-0-40-0**

38TH OVER - ROBERT CROFT 8
PAVILION END

The Surrey three-hundred comes up in style as Brown on-drives the first ball of the over high into the Lock Stand at wide long-on for a big six. The rest of the over is something of an anti-climax for the home side as each batsman picks up two on-driven singles.

MILESTONE

300 up in 37.1 overs. The sixth fifty of the innings took 34 balls.

COMPETITION RECORD

When Brown reached 181 he broke the record for the highest individual score made by a batsman against first-class opposition in a premier cup competition match, overhauling Tom Moody's unbeaten 180 for Worcestershire against Surrey at The Oval in 1994.

305-1 Ali Brown 182, Mark Ramprakash 6   *Croft 8-0-62-1*

39TH OVER - DEAN COSKER 6
VAUXHALL END

Ramprakash faces four balls and manages just two singles, while Brown, amazingly, fails to make contact with either of the deliveries he receives. His pads are in good working order, though, as two leg-byes accrue from the first of these balls and another one comes from the second. In terms of runs off the bat this is the most economical over since the third of the innings.

310-1 Ali Brown 182, Mark Ramprakash 8   *Cosker 6-0-42-0*

40TH OVER - ANDREW DAVIES 6
PAVILION END

Croft withdraws himself from the attack and reintroduces Andrew Davies. It turns out to be a fair over for the visitors, too, as Ramprakash manages a pair of twos and two ones from five balls received, while Brown drives a single to long-off from the only delivery he faces.

317-1 Ali Brown 183, Mark Ramprakash 14   *Davies 6-0-46-0*

41ST OVER - DEAN COSKER 7
VAUXHALL END

For the first four deliveries, Cosker limits the Surrey duo to a series of off-driven singles before Ramprakash forces the fifth delivery to the cover boundary. Another single, whipped to square leg, makes the over worth nine runs to Surrey.

326-1 Ali Brown 185, Mark Ramprakash 21   *Cosker 7-0-51-0*

42ND OVER - ANDREW DAVIES 7
PAVILION END

An over that starts relatively quietly, with Ramprakash driving to deep cover for a single and Brown picking off two successive twos square on the off-side, ends in explosive style as Brown smashes the last three balls for 4, 6 and 4 - an extra cover drive takes his score to 193, a pull high over midwicket takes him on to 199, then a lofted extra cover drive takes him through to a quite outstanding double-century. His innings is warmly applauded by spectators and players alike and a final Surrey total in excess of 400 now looks a mere formality.

MILESTONES

Ali Brown's second limited-overs double-century came from just 134 balls and included 10 sixes and 20 fours.

The six that Brown hit from the fifth ball of the over completed a fifty partnership for the second wicket from just 40 balls.

WORLD RECORD

Ali Brown set a new world record by becoming the first man to record two limited-overs double-centuries in first-class cricket.

345-1 Ali Brown 203, Mark Ramprakash 22   Davies 7-0-65-0

TJ - Having reached your double-century, I assume your goal now was to pass the 203 you made against Hampshire? Were you aware that Alvin Kallicharran was only just ahead of you with the record for the highest individual score in the UK?

AB - As I kept punching on and getting closer to two-hundred, I started to think that the double-hundred was on the cards and that it would be nice to pass 203 and beat my previous best, but really I just kept on batting, watching the ball and seeing it a bit bigger than when I'd started my innings! After scoring the 203 in 1997 I remembered someone telling me that I'd just missed out on the highest score made in this country but I didn't know who it was by and I wasn't thinking that I had to beat that record. And I certainly didn't know that the world record stood at 222.

TJ - So I assume you also didn't know that you had now become the first man to compile two limited-overs double-centuries in first-class cricket?

AB - No, I've read about all the records since but I had no idea at the time. For me it was just nice to beat the 203 - I've always said that if I could score 200 in forty overs then I certainly should be able to do it in fifty... with an extra ten overs anything should be possible.

43RD OVER - DARREN THOMAS 6
VAUXHALL END

It's a little surprising that Dean Cosker is withdrawn from the attack at this point, especially as his replacement is Darren Thomas, whose first five overs have cost seventy runs. After a rare dot ball to start the over, two leg-side wides and a no-ball, awarded for a full toss over waist height, don't augur too well for the rest of the over. Brown then clips to deep square leg for a single and Ramprakash drives the fourth ball over extra cover to the boundary before the Glamorgan man's luck finally changes. In trying to pull the final delivery of the over, Ramprakash miscues the ball back towards the bowler and Thomas pulls off an excellent low right-handed catch as the ball dies rapidly on him.

MILESTONE

This over saw the arrival of the Surrey 350 after 42.3 overs. The seventh fifty of the innings took 32 balls.

CAREER BEST

Brown recorded his highest limited-overs score when he reached 204, surpassing his memorable 203 v Hampshire in the Sunday League at Guildford in 1997.

22

UK AND CLUB RECORD

Upon reaching 204 Brown also improved on his own record for the highest individual score made in any limited-overs match between two first-class counties in the UK. It also bettered his own record score for a Surrey batsman, of course.

CLUB RECORD

When the score clicked over to 354, as a result of Ramprakash's boundary, Surrey recorded their highest ever total in the premier cup competition, exceeding the 350 all out they scored against Worcestershire in the epic 1994 match at the Oval.

354-2 Ali Brown 204   *Thomas 6-0-79-1*

44TH OVER - ADRIAN DALE 6
PAVILION END

With his previous over having cost nineteen runs, it is not a shock to see Davies being replaced by Dale at the pavilion end. It isn't a hugely successful move, however, as a rampant Brown drives over and through the arc between point and extra cover for 4, 2, 2, 4 after he and the new batsman, Rikki Clarke, have taken a single apiece from the first two deliveries.

UK AND COMPETITION RECORD

When Ali Brown reached 209 he recorded a new highest individual score for any limited-overs match in the United Kingdom, overhauling Alvin Kallicharran's 206 for Warwickshire v Oxfordshire at Edgbaston in the Nat West Trophy in 1984. Logically enough, it also became the highest individual score ever registered in the premier cup competition.

368-2 Ali Brown 217, Rikki Clarke 1   *Dale 7-0-57-0*

45TH OVER - DARREN THOMAS 7
VAUXHALL END

It's another very mixed over indeed from Thomas, containing a leg-side wide, two off-side wides, two singles and a two to Clarke, a single to Brown and a wicket from the final ball of the over! The wicket is that of Rikki Clarke, who top-edges an attempted upper-cut through to the keeper.

UK AND CLUB RECORD

When the total reached 376 Surrey bettered their own record for the highest score registered in any limited-overs match between two first-class counties in the United Kingdom. The previous high was the 375-4 they made against Yorkshire at Scarborough in the Sunday League in 1994.

376-3 Ali Brown 218   *Thomas 7-0-87-1*

46TH OVER - ADRIAN DALE 7
PAVILION END

Making his first appearance at The AMP Oval since his return to the country, Adam Hollioake is given a very warm reception from the crowd as he walks out to the middle. He steers his first delivery to third man for a single, having watched Brown loft the first ball over extra cover for four and drive the second to the cover sweeper for one. Once Brown is back on strike he bludgeons a straight drive powerfully down the ground to the pavilion boundary and then contents himself with a fifth-ball single, driven down to long-off.

WORLD RECORD
Upon reaching 223, Ali Brown claimed the record for the highest individual innings ever scored in a limited-overs match anywhere in the world, surpassing Graeme Pollock's unbeaten 222 for Eastern Province against Border at East London in the 1974-75 South African domestic season.

387-3 Ali Brown 228, Adam Hollioake 1   ***Dale 8-0-68-0***

47TH OVER - DARREN THOMAS 8
VAUXHALL END
Thomas goes into the record books during the over that sees Surrey pass 400. After a violent start when Brown drives through the covers for four and then upper-cuts backward of point for six, each batsman manages a brace of singles from the last four balls of the over.

MILESTONE
Surrey's 400 clicked up after 46.5 overs, with the last fifty runs having come from just 26 deliveries - the fastest fifty of an incredible innings.

CLUB RECORD
When his runs-conceded tally reached 91, after the first ball of the over, Darren Thomas became the unfortunate owner of the record for most runs conceded in any limited-overs match against Surrey, beating the 87 runs conceded by Adrian Dalby of Northumberland at Jesmond in the Nat West Trophy in 1989. Dalby's full analysis was 10-1-87-3. By the end of the over, Thomas had reached his 'ton' of runs conceded in the innings, with his century coming up at exactly the same time as Surrey's 400.

401-3 Ali Brown 240, Adam Hollioake 3   ***Thomas 8-0-101-2***

48TH OVER - ANDREW DAVIES 8
PAVILION END
After seven overs for sixty-five runs, how can things get any worse for the recalled Andrew Davies? He soon finds out as a single from the first delivery, forced to long-off by Hollioake, exposes him to the rampaging Brown. Total carnage ensues as an amazing array of strokes - a lofted extra cover drive, a pull high and wide of long-on, a cut backward of point, a flick to long leg and a drive wide of mid-on - brings a scoring sequence of 4, 6, 4, 4, 4 to add further to Davies' and Glamorgan's misery.

MILESTONE
During this incredible over, costing 23 runs, Brown passed 250 from 153 balls, including 12 sixes and 26 fours.

WORLD, UK AND COMPETITION RECORD
When the total reached 416, Surrey created a new record for the highest score made in a limited-overs match anywhere in the world, beating Somerset's 413-4 against Devon in the Nat West Trophy at Torquay in 1990. Surrey's new record was all the more impressive for the fact that the previous record total was scored in 60 overs, the duration of each innings in the premier cup competition in those days.

424-3 Ali Brown 262, Adam Hollioake 4   ***Davies 8-0-88-0***

24

49TH OVER - DARREN THOMAS 9
VAUXHALL END

A further minor consolation comes Darren Thomas's way as Hollioake skies the first ball of his ninth over to Ian Thomas at deep extra cover. With the batsmen having crossed, however, Brown is back on strike and he cuts square for four and then late for one to boost his personal tally to 267. The final three balls of the over yield just two runs, one to the new batsman, Alec Stewart, and another to Brown as the Glamorgan seamer ends on a comparative high.

WORLD, UK AND COMPETITION RECORD

The final single of the over did, however, hand Thomas the most unwanted record of all - the most expensive spell of bowling recorded in a limited-overs match anywhere in the world. His final figures of 9-0-108-3 eclipsed those of Chris Lovell (12-0-107-2) for Cornwall v Warwickshire at St Austell in 1996. Since Thomas conceded his runs in three fewer overs, he could have no arguments about becoming the new record holder.

431-4 Ali Brown 268, Alec Stewart 1   *Thomas 9-0-108-3*

50TH OVER - MICHAEL KASPROWICZ 10
PAVILION END

Brown's monumental innings ends with the first ball of the final over when he steps across his stumps and has his off stump knocked back by a very good yorker from the returning Kasprowicz. He leaves the field to a great reception from the smallish crowd, accepting the congratulations of a number of his opponents on the way. The remaining five deliveries of the innings bring an edged boundary and two singles to Jon Batty plus a single for Alec Stewart. Just seven runs have come from the final over but that hardly seems to matter given the enormous total already on the board.

WORLD RECORD

The new world record for a limited-overs innings total was therefore finally set at 438-5 and the individual score at 268. Ali Brown's innings lasted 160 balls and contained 12 sixes and 30 fours.

438-5 Alec Stewart 2, Jon Batty 6   *Kasprowicz 10-0-53-1*

TJ - The Glamorgan players seemed very generous in their praise - Kasprowicz patted you on the back as you passed him and I also noted that Darren Thomas shook your hand. Nice gestures, I thought.

AB - Yes, a few nice things were said to me, though I couldn't remember exactly what they were right now. I've known a number of their players for quite some time and they are an excellent side as they proved by winning division one of the Norwich Union League - it shows what you can do when you play positive cricket.

TJ - One of the most amazing features of the Surrey innings for me was that the Glamorgan ground fielding was actually very good throughout. Would you agree with that assessment?

AB - Yes, they did field well but we were quite piercing with our boundary shots and they would have needed some very tall fielders to stop some of the sixes! Of the thirty fours and twelve sixes I hit, I don't recall any coming as a result of a *piece of bad fielding. Mind you, my timing was so good that day that I'd hit, say, an extra cover drive and think 'I've hit that well' - then a couple of seconds later, as it hit the boundary boards, I'd be thinking 'I hit that **really** well!'... so perhaps at times we didn't give them a chance to show how good their fielding was!*

TJ - I assume you would nominate Kasprowicz as the best Glamorgan bowler during the innings?

AB - Yes, he's an international bowler and he bowled very well - it swung a bit in the early stages and he put the ball in the right areas. But it wasn't a very forgiving wicket for the bowlers - you could sometimes bowl a good ball that would still get hit for a boundary.

TJ - I guess you must have been pretty tired after almost fifty overs at the crease playing such a high-tempo innings?

AB - Not especially, no, I don't tend to get too tired - the only thing I've found tiring this year is looking after my young son! It does help when you get the majority of your runs in boundaries but I think the adrenaline keeps you going and stops you feeling tired. I also tend to have good aerobic fitness and I'm used to playing long innings. During the 203 I started to cramp up a little bit in my wrists but here I felt fine and I think I could have batted for another fifty overs.

TJ - At the time, as you were leaving the pitch and as you were sat down between the innings, could you fully appreciate what you had just achieved?

AB - Similar to the 203, I came into the dressing and people looked at me as if to say 'What have you just done?' but, to me, I'm a batsman and scoring runs is what I'm there to do. But I realised it was special when everyone came into the dressing room, almost in a single line, to congratulate me. I think maybe I appreciate the achievement more now than I did at the time.

SURREY innings							
Fall of wkt	Batsman	How	Out	Score	Balls	4s	6s
1-286	I.J. Ward		b Croft	97	95	8	4
5-431	A.D. Brown		b Kasprowicz	268	160	30	12
2-354	M.R. Ramprakash	c &	b S.D. Thomas	26	27	2	0
3-376	R.R. Clarke	c Wallace	b S.D. Thomas	5	6	0	0
4-424	A.J. Hollioake *	c I.J. Thomas	b S.D. Thomas	4	6	0	0
	A.J. Stewart	Not	Out	2	4	0	0
	J.N. Batty +	Not	Out	6	3	1	0
	M.P. Bicknell	Did not bat					
	Saqlain Mushtaq	Did not bat					
	J. Ormond	Did not bat					
	E.S.H. Giddins	Did not bat					
	Extras	(8lb, 20w, 2nb)		30			
TOTAL	(50 overs)		(for 5 wickets)	438			

Kasprowicz	10	0	53	1
Davies	8	0	88	0
S.D. Thomas	9	0	108	3
Croft	8	0	62	1
Dale	8	0	68	0
Cosker	7	0	51	0

And so Glamorgan set out to chase the apparently theoretical target of 439 to win the match. It represented the most daunting challenge faced by any side in the history of limited-overs cricket...

1ST OVER - MARTIN BICKNELL 1
VAUXHALL END

Facing mission impossible, Robert Croft gets Glamorgan off to a rousing start by crashing the first five balls of the innings to the boundary, with a variety of well executed strokes - a slash over backward point, a drive wide of mid-on, a force through extra cover, a lofted drive over mid-off and a sliced drive backward of point. Much to the relief of the bowler, Croft fails to score from the final ball.

20-0 Robert Croft 20, Ian Thomas 0   *Bicknell 1-0-20-0*

TJ - Could you believe your eyes when Bickers' first five deliveries were smashed to the boundary?

AB - I got the feeling we were a bit complacent - we knew we had a massive score on the board, a world record, and probably felt there was no way they were getting that total. But all credit to them because that start made it immediately obvious that they weren't coming out just to play for their figures, they were out there to try to win. They had a plan and the wicket was very good. I think our bowlers were under the impression that if they simply bowled a good length then eventually the batsmen would nick one or hit one up in the air but when Crofty hit Bickers' first five half-volleys and long-hops for four we were immediately thinking 'Hang on a minute, if it rains suddenly they are ahead of the rate'!

2ND OVER - ED GIDDINS 1
PAVILION END

Following the example of his stand-in captain, Ian Thomas also gets away to a flying start, picking up his first delivery for a six backward of square leg and then whipping his third ball through midwicket for three. Back on strike, Croft makes it seven boundaries from eight balls faced when he hits his first ball from Giddins back down the ground over the bowler's head and then crashes a drive through extra cover. Although the final ball of the over is, again, a very welcome dot ball for Surrey, the Welshmen have notched an amazing thirty-seven runs from just twelve balls.

37-0 Robert Croft 28, Ian Thomas 9   *Giddins 1-0-17-0*

3RD OVER - MARTIN BICKNELL 2
VAUXHALL END

Some sanity returns to proceedings as only six runs, including a whipped boundary through midwicket by Croft, accrue from the over. The Glamorgan skipper enjoys a stroke of good fortune when he miscues the fourth ball high into space on the off-side. With no fielder able to reach the ball, he profits by a single, however.

43-0 Robert Croft 33, Ian Thomas 10   *Bicknell 2-0-26-0*

4TH OVER - ED GIDDINS 2
PAVILION END

Croft is quickly back on the attack, slicing the first ball to the rope backward of point and then bringing up the Glamorgan fifty next ball by driving a full-toss through extra cover for another boundary. With the visiting captain having forced the fifth ball to mid-off for a single to relinquish the strike, Thomas then completes an eleven-run over by edging the final delivery to third man for two.

MILESTONE

50 up/50 partnership in an incredible 3.2 overs (20 balls).

CAREER BEST

Ian Thomas' previous best score in the premier cup competition - 11 v Somerset at Taunton in 2001 - was passed with the two he scored from the last ball of the over.

54-0 Robert Croft 42, Ian Thomas 12   *Giddins 2-0-28-0*

5TH OVER - MARTIN BICKNELL 3
VAUXHALL END

After Croft smashes Bicknell's opening delivery back over his head to the rope, the rest of the over sees just three singles being added to the visitors' total. In the circumstances it represents something of a triumph for the bowler.

61-0 Robert Croft 48, Ian Thomas 13   *Bicknell 3-0-33-0*

6TH OVER - JIMMY ORMOND 1
PAVILION END

Jimmy Ormond replaces Giddins at the pavilion end but gets off to the worst possible start as Croft drives his first ball over wide long-on for six to complete a stunning half-century from just 22 deliveries. He loses the strike next ball when he miscues into the leg-side for a single but this doesn't help Ormond since Thomas cuts the fifth ball of the over for four and lifts the sixth over mid-on for another boundary. The over costs fifteen as Glamorgan's whirlwind start continues.

MILESTONE

Robert Croft's fifty came from a mere 22 balls, including 1 six and 11 fours.

76-0 Robert Croft 55, Ian Thomas 21   *Ormond 1-0-15-0*

7TH OVER - MARTIN BICKNELL 4
VAUXHALL END

For the sixth time in the first seven overs the opening delivery yields a boundary as Croft's drive beats the fielder at wide mid-on. Bicknell again regains a little control in the rest of the over, though, conceding just three singles, two to Croft and one to Thomas.

83-0 Robert Croft 61, Ian Thomas 22   *Bicknell 4-0-40-0*

8TH OVER - JIMMY ORMOND 2
PAVILION END

Finally, a Surrey bowler manages to start his over with a dot ball... then the Glamorgan skipper hooks the second delivery for six! He follows up by picking up two more runs with a cut backward of point next ball, before Ormond exerts a tighter grip, conceding just one run from the final three deliveries.

CAREER BEST

Robert Croft posted his highest score in the premier cup competition when the six at the start of the over moved his tally on to 67. His previous best was the 64 he made against Bedfordshire at Cardiff in 1997.

92-0 Robert Croft 70, Ian Thomas 22   *Ormond 2-0-24-0*

9TH OVER - SAQLAIN MUSHTAQ 1
VAUXHALL END

With his three frontline seamers unable to contain the Glamorgan openers, Adam Hollioake takes the sensible, if slightly risky, option of changing the pace of the bowling by introducing Saqlain Mushtaq. Croft immediately makes it clear that he is not going to shirk this challenge, driving the off-spinner's second ball over long-off for six, cutting the next delivery for two to raise the Glamorgan hundred in double-quick time, and then pushing the following ball through midwicket for another two. A single to point from the final delivery completes an eleven-run over which gives the Surrey captain more food for thought.

MILESTONE
100 up/100 partnership in just 8.3 overs (51 balls). The second fifty of the innings required just 31 deliveries.

103-0 Robert Croft 81, Ian Thomas 22   *Saqlain 1-0-11-0*

10TH OVER - JIMMY ORMOND 3
PAVILION END

Croft's blistering assault continues as Ormond is driven square and pulled over mid-on for two more boundaries from his first three balls. The second half of the over brings just a single apiece for the two batsmen but the over still costs ten. It's the sixth over of the innings to yield ten or more runs already.

113-0 Robert Croft 90, Ian Thomas 23   *Ormond 3-0-34-0*

11TH OVER - SAQLAIN MUSHTAQ 2
VAUXHALL END

The breakthrough that Surrey are so desperately seeking comes when Ian Thomas is run out in attempting a run from the first ball of the over. Having driven hard to deepish mid-off and seen Adam Hollioake misfield momentarily, he sets off for a run. The Surrey captain recovers rapidly, however, and his venomous throw to the non-striker's end shatters the stumps with Thomas still short of his ground. Almost inevitably, the loss of this wicket gives Surrey some breathing space as the remaining five balls of the over bring just an on-driven single to Croft.

114-1 Robert Croft 91, David Hemp 0   *Saqlain 2-0-12-0*

12TH OVER - JIMMY ORMOND 4
PAVILION END

Despite Glamorgan's withering assault on them, the Surrey bowlers have at least been keeping a reasonable line because the first wide of the innings - the first extra of any type, in fact - arrives at the start of this, the twelfth, over. For once Croft is kept in check, the only scoring strokes being a thick-edged four and a push into the covers for one. A leg-bye from the last ball immediately doubles the extras count.

121-1 Robert Croft 96, David Hemp 0   *Ormond 4-0-40-0*

TJ - Although the Glamorgan target was huge and still miles away, were there any uneasy feelings at this relatively early stage? What more, if anything, could the bowlers have done?

AB - We knew they would have a real crack in the first fifteen overs but then hoped things would slow down once we could move a few fielders out. It was worrying that we kept bowling length deliveries, hoping for a 'cheap' wicket, if you like - we didn't really bowl enough blockhole balls or change our pace as much as we could have done.

13TH OVER - SAQLAIN MUSHTAQ 3
VAUXHALL END

Having conceded just a single from his previous over, Saqlain follows up with a three-run second over, conceding just a single for a clip backward of square leg to David Hemp and a two clipped over midwicket by Croft.

124-1 Robert Croft 98, David Hemp 1   ***Saqlain 3-0-15-0***

14TH OVER - JIMMY ORMOND 5
PAVILION END

Although Ormond manages another boundary-free over, Hemp is able to pick off a two to square leg and a single to cover, while Croft picks up two singles, one to mid-off and another to third man. The second of these takes the stand-in captain through to a breathtaking century from just 56 deliveries. A leg-side wide and a leg-bye also accrue from a seven-run over.

MILESTONE

Robert Croft's first century in this competition, and his second in all limited-overs cricket, came from only 56 deliveries and included 3 sixes and 15 fours.

CLUB RECORD

Croft's century became the fastest ever scored by a Glamorgan batsman in limited-overs cricket, beating, by two balls, Matthew Maynard's 58-ball ton against British Universities at Cambridge in the Benson & Hedges Cup in 1996.

131-1 Robert Croft 100, David Hemp 4   ***Ormond 5-0-46-0***

15TH OVER - SAQLAIN MUSHTAQ 4
VAUXHALL END

Having conceded just four runs from his previous two overs, Saqlain suddenly feels the Glamorgan lash again as Croft launches him wide of mid-on and then straight for fours from the second and third balls of the over. After the Glamorgan skipper miscues the next ball backward of square leg for a single, Hemp adds to Saqlain's discomfort with a swept boundary and a single to midwicket to complete an expensive over costing fourteen runs. The first fifteen overs of the innings have yielded an incredible 145 runs, leaving Adam Hollioake hoping that the lifting of the fielding restrictions will help to slow down the scoring rate.

145-1 Robert Croft 109, David Hemp 9   ***Saqlain 4-0-29-0***

16TH OVER - ADAM HOLLIOAKE 1
PAVILION END

The Surrey skipper brings himself into the firing line and starts well, with just three singles coming from the first four balls of his over. Croft then ruins his opposite number's good start by forcing the next ball to the long-off boundary to bring up the Glamorgan 150 and then driving a single to deep cover to end the over.

MILESTONE

150 up in 15.5 overs, with the last fifty having arrived in a comparatively sedate 44 balls.

CAREER BEST

Robert Croft beat his previous highest score in all limited-overs cricket when reaching 115. Before today his best score had been the 114 not out he scored against Middlesex at Cardiff in the National League in 2001.

153-1 Robert Croft 115, David Hemp 11   *Hollioake 1-0-8-0*

17TH OVER - JIMMY ORMOND 6
VAUXHALL END

A fine over from Ormond almost brings the second breakthrough that Surrey seek as Croft top-edges the first ball towards Ed Giddins at long-leg. It looks likely to be a fairly routine catch but the fielder is slow off the mark and barely gets a hand to the ball as it falls safely to earth just inches in front of him. The single that the batsmen scamper is a very fortunate one, as is the run gained by Hemp when he digs out a yorker two balls later. A pair of authentic cover drives, one by each batsman and each worth just one run, complete a good over for Surrey.

157-1 Robert Croft 117, David Hemp 13   *Ormond 6-0-50-0*

18TH OVER - ADAM HOLLIOAKE 2
PAVILION END

After Hemp takes three runs from the first two deliveries, Croft lofts the ball into space on the leg-side for a further two runs before falling victim to Adam Hollioake's slower ball to provide much needed relief for Surrey. The fifth ball of the over sees the Glamorgan captain skying high into the covers where Ian Ward completes the catch. Croft's outstanding innings of 119 from 69 balls has given his team a wonderful start, even though their task remains positively gargantuan. With the batsmen having crossed while the ball was in the air, Hemp squeezes the final ball of the over down to long leg for a single.

163-2 David Hemp 17, Matthew Maynard 0   *Hollioake 2-0-14-1*

TJ - That really was some innings by Robert Croft. The best you've seen him bat? AB - Yes, I'd say so. I've seen him bat many times - he takes a good step back and he was always setting himself to have a big heave but he's got a good eye and he strikes the ball very cleanly. He played very well.

19TH OVER - JIMMY ORMOND 7
VAUXHALL END

The over starts well for Surrey with Hemp only able to pick up a single from the first three balls but Matthew Maynard drives his first ball wide of mid-on for four and then moves his score up to five with another run to extra cover from the final delivery of the over. A six-run over represents success for Surrey since Glamorgan still need almost nine runs per over to win at this stage.

169-2 David Hemp 18, Matthew Maynard 5   *Ormond 7-0-56-0*

20TH OVER - ADAM HOLLIOAKE 3
PAVILION END

It's another decent over for the home side as their skipper concedes just a single from each of the first five deliveries and then finishes off with a dot ball.

174-2 David Hemp 20, Matthew Maynard 8   *Hollioake 3-0-19-1*

21ST OVER - JIMMY ORMOND 8
VAUXHALL END

Ormond is out of luck again as a good over ends up costing seven runs. Maynard looks comfortable as he pulls the opening delivery to long leg for one run and guides the fifth to third man for another single but Hemp is fortunate as he miscues the fourth ball to square leg for one and thick edges the final delivery to the third man boundary.

181-2 David Hemp 25, Matthew Maynard 10   *Ormond 8-0-63-0*

22ND OVER - ADAM HOLLIOAKE 4
PAVILION END

Hemp is much more assured in the next over from Hollioake, forcing the second ball backward of point for four and driving to deep point for a single from the fourth. Maynard tops and tails the over with confident strokes to midwicket for one run apiece. Glamorgan have scored seven from the over, so honours are just about even between bowler and batsmen.

188-2 David Hemp 30, Matthew Maynard 12   *Hollioake 4-0-26-1*

23RD OVER - JIMMY ORMOND 9
VAUXHALL END

With the required run rate now touching nine, Glamorgan are grateful to Maynard for finding the rope twice in this over, firstly with an on-drive and then with a pull wide of mid-on. The former captain adds a further run with a clip to deep square leg to ensure that his side hits their target for this over at least.

197-2 David Hemp 30, Matthew Maynard 21   *Ormond 9-0-72-0*

24TH OVER - ED GIDDINS 3
PAVILION END

After four respectable overs in the context of the match Adam Hollioake removes himself from the attack, doubtless wishing to save the rest of his overs for the end of the innings. Ed Giddins now returns to the fray after his wretched first spell of two overs for twenty-eight runs and immediately goes some way to making amends by removing the dangerous Maynard with his third delivery. To be honest, it's a dreadful long hop, pulled straight down the throat of Ramprakash at deep midwicket, that brings the breakthrough but, after the visitors' flying start, Surrey are grateful for any wicket no matter how it comes about. With the batsmen having crossed, Adrian Dale steers his second ball to third man before a leg-bye completes the over. A very satisfactory one it has been for Surrey and Giddins, too - just two runs and an all-important wicket.

199-3 David Hemp 30, Adrian Dale 1   *Giddins 3-0-29-1*

25TH OVER - MARTIN BICKNELL 5
VAUXHALL END

It's a double change as Ormond is, perhaps surprisingly, taken off with just one over of his allotted ten still to bowl. His replacement is Martin Bicknell, who, like Giddins, had suffered something of a mauling at the start of the innings. Surrey's 'Mr Reliable' starts his second spell well, however, with just a single to Hemp coming from the opening three balls before Dale lofts the next delivery over extra cover for four runs. It's an ambitious shot from what is only the fourth ball he has faced but it's perfectly executed and shows what a very good batting track this match is being played on. A drive to deep point brings a single from the fifth ball of the over before Bicknell completes a satisfactory return to the attack with a 'maiden ball'. Despite their fantastic efforts to date, at the halfway stage of their reply Glamorgan still need a daunting 234 runs at a rate of 9.36 per over.

MILESTONE

200 up in 24.2 overs, with the fourth fifty of Glamorgan's reply having come up in 51 balls, making it the slowest of the innings by some distance.

205-3 David Hemp 31, Adrian Dale 6   ***Bicknell 5-0-46-0***

TJ - To be honest, I'd expected Glamorgan to be out of the game by the halfway stage of their innings, yet they were almost halfway to their target with seven wickets still standing. Were you surprised that they were so well placed, too?

AB - I know that I didn't feel secure until the end of the final over. Every time we bowled a good over there seemed to be a six at the end of it, so we had to be on our toes all the way. After the great start they had I certainly didn't think we could coast home at any stage.

26TH OVER - ED GIDDINS 4
PAVILION END

The good work of Giddins' promising comeback over is soon undone as he is savaged for seventeen runs in the second over of his new spell. After Dale has nudged the first delivery to third man for a single, Hemp drives over mid-on for a boundary and then hits the next ball straight for one, leaving Dale to end the over in style. The Glamorgan all-rounder pulls the fourth delivery for six over midwicket, drives the next just over the head of a leaping mid-off for four and finishes the over with a simple push backward of point for a single.

222-3 David Hemp 36, Adrian Dale 18   ***Giddins 4-0-46-1***

27TH OVER - MARTIN BICKNELL 6
VAUXHALL END

The next over, from Bicknell, is a much tighter one. A pair of on-driven singles, one to each batsman, give Surrey the advantage at the halfway point of the over but Glamorgan regain a little of the lost ground when Dale's slightly edgy late cut finds the rope at third man from the fourth delivery. A leg-glance for one ends the over with Bicknell feeling rather more satisfied than the batsmen.

229-3 David Hemp 37, Adrian Dale 24   ***Bicknell 6-0-53-0***

28TH OVER - ED GIDDINS 5
PAVILION END

The twenty-eighth over follows much the same pattern as the previous one, with a boundary from the fourth ball - an on-drive by Hemp - slightly spoiling an otherwise tight over. A leg-bye, two singles to Hemp and one to Dale supplement the four, making the over worth eight runs - still below the required rate which stands at 9.18 by the end of the over.

237-3 David Hemp 43, Adrian Dale 25   ***Giddins 5-0-53-1***

29TH OVER - MARTIN BICKNELL 7
VAUXHALL END

Just two singles to Hemp and one to Dale accrue from the first five balls before the latter ruins Bicknell's fine over by lofting a drive to the rope wide of mid-on. It's still a fair over from Surrey's point of view, but it would clearly have been much better without that last-ball boundary.

244-3 David Hemp 45, Adrian Dale 30   *Bicknell 7-0-60-0*

30TH OVER - RIKKI CLARKE 1
PAVILION END

Giddins is removed from the firing line again and replaced by Rikki Clarke, who produces an excellent opening over. In the context of this match it is almost a miracle that the young Surrey all-rounder concedes just two singles - a square drive by Hemp and an off-drive by Dale - from his first six deliveries of the contest. Glamorgan can't afford too many more overs like this one.

246-3 David Hemp 46, Adrian Dale 31   *Clarke 1-0-2-0*

31ST OVER - MARTIN BICKNELL 8
VAUXHALL END

They fare little better in the next over, however, as Bicknell's accuracy restricts them to just three singles - two to Dale and one to Hemp. Perhaps significantly, with 190 runs now needed from nineteen overs, the required run rate has reached ten for the first time in the innings.

MILESTONE
The first single taken from the over completed a 50-run partnership in just 41 balls.

249-3 David Hemp 47, Adrian Dale 33   *Bicknell 8-0-63-0*

32ND OVER - RIKKI CLARKE 2
PAVILION END

Glamorgan receive a much-needed boost when Dale pulls the opening ball of Clarke's second over to the midwicket fence. Luckily for Surrey, Clarke regains some of the lost ground by yielding just five singles - mainly through pushes to mid-on and midwicket - from the remainder of the over.

MILESTONE
250 up in 31.1 overs. The last fifty was therefore scored from 41 deliveries.

258-3 David Hemp 49, Adrian Dale 40   *Clarke 2-0-11-0*

33RD OVER - SAQLAIN MUSHTAQ 5
VAUXHALL END

Having completed a well-controlled second spell of 4-0-23-0, Bicknell is replaced at the Vauxhall end by Saqlain Mushtaq. This move seems to suit the Welsh pair as they plunder ten runs with relative ease, Dale's square-cut boundary from the fifth delivery boosting the tally from an over which otherwise produces five singles and a leg-side wide.

MILESTONE
Hemp completed a half-century from 60 balls with his first single in this over. He registered just 5 fours in reaching the landmark.

268-3 David Hemp 51, Adrian Dale 47   *Saqlain 5-0-39-0*

34

34TH OVER - RIKKI CLARKE 3
PAVILION END

Clarke pays a heavy price for bowling a little too short in his third over, Hemp pulling the third and fourth balls backward of square leg and then over midwicket respectively for boundary fours. These lapses ruin an over which otherwise yields just two singles, one to each batsman.

UK AND COMPETITION RECORD

The record for the highest match aggregate registered in any limited-overs match in the UK fell when Glamorgan reached 272. The 710 runs so far scored in the match surpassed the 707-run aggregate managed by Worcestershire (357-2) and Surrey (350) in their Nat West Trophy match at The Oval in 1994.

278-3 David Hemp 60, Adrian Dale 48   *Clarke 3-0-21-0*

35TH OVER - SAQLAIN MUSHTAQ 6
VAUXHALL END

A violent assault on Saqlain sees Hemp stepping on the accelerator with 161 needed from sixteen overs. After failing to score from the first ball, successive slog-sweeps for six - the second carrying over the short boundary despite having been miscued - make it Glamorgan's over with three balls left to bowl. Hemp adds to the Surrey off-spinner's misery by sweeping conventionally for two and one from the next two deliveries, before a leg-side wide and a single to Dale end a very good over for the visitors. The required run rate has dropped below ten again following this seventeen-run over.

295-3 David Hemp 75, Adrian Dale 49   *Saqlain 6-0-56-0*

36TH OVER - ADAM HOLLIOAKE 5
PAVILION END

With Glamorgan's consistent progress and sudden acceleration causing increasing concern amongst the Surrey faithful, Adam Hollioake returns to the attack and immediately appears to turn things around with two wickets in three balls. The first delivery of his new spell sees Dale poking a simple catch to Clarke at cover, ending an excellent knock one run short of fifty, then, two balls later, the new batsman, Michael Powell, drives loosely to Giddins at deep mid-on. Surrey players and fans breathe a sigh of relief in the hope that the Glamorgan surge might be fatally slowed by the loss of these wickets but, following a leg-side wide, Darren Thomas immediately opens his account with an off-driven single. The extras tally rises further with two leg-byes before Hemp whips the last ball of the over to square leg for the run that raises his side's 300.

MILESTONE

300 up in 36.0 overs. A mere 29 balls were needed for the latest fifty of the innings.

300-5 David Hemp 76, Darren Thomas 1   *Hollioake 5-0-29-3*

37TH OVER - RIKKI CLARKE 4
VAUXHALL END

Having been switched to the Vauxhall end, Rikki Clarke starts well, keeping the ball up to the bat and conceding four singles from drives down the ground from his first four balls. Hemp lofts the next delivery back over the bowler's head for a boundary, however, and a cover-driven single from ball six leaves the over costing nine runs to keep Glamorgan up with the asking rate.

CLUB RECORD
When the score reached 308 Glamorgan set a new mark for their highest score when batting second in the premier cup competition, the previous best being the 304-8 they racked up against Hampshire at Southampton in 1997.

309-5 David Hemp 82, Darren Thomas 4   *Clarke 4-0-30-0*

38TH OVER - SAQLAIN MUSHTAQ 7
PAVILION END

Saqlain has also switched ends, which seems to be a sensible move since there are two left-handers at the crease and the short boundary is now at backward point rather than wide mid-on, where Hemp had slog-swept two sixes in the off-spinner's last over from the Vauxhall end. The first two balls are swept for singles, before Hemp pushes to cover for one run and, after a dot ball, Thomas ends the over with an on-drive for two and a top-edged sweep for a single. A total of six runs from the over represents a good return for Surrey since it pushes the required run rate back over ten.

CLUB RECORD
The end-of-over total, 315, set a new mark for the highest score ever posted by Glamorgan when batting second in a limited-overs match, beating the 314-2 they had amassed against British Universities at Cambridge in the Benson & Hedges Cup in 1996.

315-5 David Hemp 84, Darren Thomas 8   *Saqlain 7-0-62-0*

39TH OVER - ADAM HOLLIOAKE 6
VAUXHALL END

Rikki Clarke's return has been short-lived as Adam Hollioake switches to the Vauxhall end for his third spell of the innings. He concedes just an on-driven single to Darren Thomas from his opening two deliveries but then all hell breaks loose as Hemp registers 4, 4, 6 from balls three to five, courtesy of a lofted on-drive, an extra cover drive and a soaring on-drive. Another drive, this time for a single to midwicket, ends a very productive sixteen-run over for the visitors.

WORLD RECORD
When Glamorgan reached 320 another new record was set - the highest match aggregate ever recorded in a first-class limited-overs match anywhere in the world. The previous record of 754 runs (India 392-6 v India B 362 at Chennai in 2000/01) had been eclipsed with more than eleven overs of the second innings of the match still to be bowled!

CLUB RECORD
At the same point Glamorgan registered their highest total against a first-class county in any limited-overs match, surpassing the 316-8 they compiled against Essex at Cardiff in the Nat West Trophy in 1994.

331-5 David Hemp 99, Darren Thomas 9   *Hollioake 6-0-45-3*

40TH OVER - SAQLAIN MUSHTAQ 8
PAVILION END

Hemp completes the day's third magnificent century with a push to square cover for a single from the opening delivery of the over. The next five balls are good from a Surrey point of view, with a dot ball followed by four singles, one pushed to mid-on and the other three swept backward of square leg. With ten overs left to bowl, Glamorgan now require 103 runs… a very tough but certainly not impossible target, especially if the flying Hemp can stick around.

MILESTONE

David Hemp's century came up in 85 balls with 3 sixes and 10 fours. The second fifty runs of his innings had come from an amazing 25 deliveries.

336-5 David Hemp 102, Darren Thomas 11   *Saqlain 8-0-67-0*

41ST OVER - MARTIN BICKNELL 9
VAUXHALL END

Unfortunately for Glamorgan, Hemp departs to the first ball of a new spell from Martin Bicknell, who has replaced his skipper in the firing line. Hemp's dismissal for an excellent 102 comes about when he splices a pull shot to provide wide mid-on with a straightforward catch. Could this prove to be the final fatal blow for the brave Welshmen? Unsurprisingly, things are a little subdued for the rest of the over with just five singles picked off, three by the new batsman, Mark Wallace, and two by Thomas. The required run rate is now nigh on eleven an over.

341-6 Darren Thomas 13, Mark Wallace 3   *Bicknell 9-0-68-1*

42ND OVER - SAQLAIN MUSHTAQ 9
PAVILION END

There's a nervy moment for Wallace as he miscues the first ball of the over into space at cover for a single. Thomas shows no such uncertainty, though, as he slog-sweeps and reverse sweeps fours from the next two deliveries before settling for a single to long-off from the fourth ball. Wallace forces the last delivery to extra cover to complete an eleven-run over for the visitors and maintain their outside chance of pulling off a truly remarkable victory.

UK AND COMPETITION RECORD

When they passed 350, Glamorgan beat the record for the highest team total recorded by a side batting second in any first-class limited-overs match in the UK. The previous holders were, ironically, Surrey who scored 350 against Worcestershire at the Oval in the Nat West Trophy in 1994.

MILESTONE

350 up in 41.3 overs. Another rapid fifty had arrived in a mere 33 deliveries.

352-6 Darren Thomas 22, Mark Wallace 5   *Saqlain 9-0-78-0*

43RD OVER - MARTIN BICKNELL 10
VAUXHALL END

The trusty 'Bickers' does the trick for Surrey again as he makes another breakthrough, the first ball of his final over bringing the wicket of Wallace who skies the ball high to Mark Ramprakash stationed on the deep midwicket boundary. At this point, with the visitors now running out of wickets, the home side look

37

strong favourites again but by the end of the over the odds have shifted once more as no fewer than sixteen runs come from the final five balls of Bicknell's ten-over allocation. With the batsmen having crossed as Wallace was caught, Thomas pulls the second ball of the over for one run before Kasprowicz gets off to a great start with a leg-glanced boundary and an off-driven single from balls three and four. Thomas then ensures that Bicknell will wish to forget this spell quickly by smashing the fifth delivery over wide mid-on for six and forcing the last ball to the rope at extra cover. As the battered 'Bickers' retires to the outfield with figures of 10-0-84-2, Glamorgan now need 71 runs from seven overs.

WORLD RECORD

At 364 Glamorgan posted a new world-best for the highest team total recorded by a side batting second in any first-class limited-overs match. India B's 362 against India at Chennai in 2000/01 had bitten the dust, like so many other records in this amazing match.

CLUB RECORD

Martin Bicknell's final bowling analysis became the most expensive for Surrey in any limited-overs match, overtaking two spells by Robin Jackman, the first of 8-0-78-2 against Middlesex at The Oval in the Sunday League in 1971 and the second of 11-0-78-1 against Kent, also at The Oval, in the Benson & Hedges Cup in 1973. There was still time for some of Bicknell's colleagues to 'beat' the new record during the rest of the innings, however!

368-7 Darren Thomas 33, Michael Kasprowicz 5   *Bicknell 10-0-84-2*

44TH OVER - SAQLAIN MUSHTAQ 10
PAVILION END

Starting his last over with figures of 9-0-78-0, Saqlain looks likely to break Bicknell's unwanted record straight away but he produces an excellent over, restricting the Glamorgan duo to a brace of singles each. With 67 runs now needed from just 36 balls (11.17 per over) Surrey appear to have just a little leeway at last… though the nature of this game suggests that it might still be too early for the home side to feel safe.

372-7 Darren Thomas 35, Michael Kasprowicz 7   *Saqlain 10-0-82-0*

TJ - If someone had said to you at the start of the day that both Bickers and Saqi would concede eighty-plus runs in their ten-over allocations what would your response have been?

AB - It would have surprised me but I would probably have been more surprised about Saqi. Once we'd batted, because the wicket was so good and because there was one shortish boundary, I would have thought there was always a chance of one or more of the bowlers suffering. On a good wicket like that you need to use a lot of changes of pace and I don't think Bickers did that often enough. To be fair, though, it was always likely to be difficult for any bowler in these conditions. What you can say in their defence is that they both ended up conceding fewer runs per over than Glamorgan had needed to win the match at the start of their innings!

45TH OVER - ED GIDDINS 6
VAUXHALL END

With his two most reliable bowlers having now completed their spells, Adam Hollioake looks set to turn back to Jimmy Ormond until Ed Giddins approaches his skipper and initiates a conversation, the upshot of which is that Giddins takes the ball. In desperate need of a high-scoring over to keep his team in the game, Thomas obliges by taking ten runs from the first three balls of the over - a streaky edge past his leg stump for four is sandwiched by two very authentic strokes, an off-driven two and an on-drive to the boundary. Giddins regains his composure, however, yielding just two singles - an on-driven single to Thomas and a leg-glance to Kasprowicz - in the second half of the over. Glamorgan require fifty-five runs from five overs, but have at least fractionally reduced the required rate as a result of taking twelve runs from this over.

CAREER BEST

When Darren Thomas' score reached 41 he registered a new highest score in all limited-overs cricket, beating the 40 he made against the Hampshire Cricket Board at Southampton in the Nat West Trophy in 1999.

CLUB RECORD

When the Glamorgan total clicked up to 374 it became the highest recorded by the Welsh county in any limited-overs match, passing the previous best of 373-7 against Bedfordshire at Cardiff in the Nat West Trophy in 1998.

384-7 Darren Thomas 46, Michael Kasprowicz 8   ***Giddins 6-0-65-1***

TJ - Five overs to go, fifty-five runs required. Do you remember what you were thinking and how you were feeling at that stage?

AB - I still didn't feel comfortable - there were still too many balls flying over my head for me to feel at ease!

46TH OVER - ADAM HOLLIOAKE 7
PAVILION END

The enforced bowling change at the pavilion end sees Adam Hollioake reappearing for his fourth spell of the innings. From a Surrey point of view he starts well with drives to deep cover and long-off from the first two balls earning just one run apiece. A leg-bye is then all the Glamorgan duo can manage from ball three, before a pair of on-driven singles bring us to the final delivery with just five scored from the over. Clearly in need of something special, Thomas rises to the occasion, thumping the ball back over Hollioake's head for a superb straight six to complete an excellent half-century in double-quick time. Twenty-four balls remain, forty-four runs are needed and, given the way Thomas is batting, it still seems possible.

MILESTONE

Darren Thomas completed his half-century from 30 balls with 2 sixes and 5 fours.

395-7 Darren Thomas 54, Michael Kasprowicz 10   ***Hollioake 7-0-55-3***

47TH OVER - ED GIDDINS 7
VAUXHALL END

It's all to play for as Giddins begins the forty-seventh over. Kasprowicz claims a single by driving the opening delivery to cover then Thomas follows suit with a drive to long-on from ball two. The third delivery is a fine yorker but Kasprowicz digs it out and the batsmen scramble through for another single. It's advantage Giddins at this point, a fact clearly acknowledged by Thomas as his desperate slog at the next ball demonstrates, though it does earn him two runs to midwicket. A much better stroke through extra cover earns him two further runs from the fifth delivery but he is then unable to score from the last ball of what has been a good over under pressure. Surrey are very happy with a seven-run over which pushes Glamorgan's requirement up to greater than two runs per ball - 37 from 18.

MILESTONE

Glamorgan's 400 arrived after 46.4 overs, just one ball quicker than Surrey's 400. The last fifty runs have taken 31 deliveries.

A fifty partnership (from just 28 balls) between Thomas and Kasprowicz was completed one ball after the 400 came up.

402-7 Darren Thomas 59, Michael Kasprowicz 12　　　　　*Giddins 7-0-72-1*

48TH OVER - ADAM HOLLIOAKE 8
PAVILION END

Just as it seems Glamorgan have too much to do they hit back in style as Kasprowicz clubs the first ball of Hollioake's over, a full toss, over the midwicket boundary for six. What a difference that one shot makes, bringing the visitors' requirement down to 31 runs from 17 balls - suddenly it looks on again. Fortunately for Surrey, Hollioake claws back a little ground as the big Australian fails to score from his second delivery and can only manage a single to long-on from the next, putting Thomas back on strike. The left-hander cannot get the fourth ball away but a mixture of bat and pad sees the ball dribble away to midwicket for a single. The pressure is back on Kasprowicz... but only for a moment as he cleverly steers ball five between two single-saving fielders to the third man boundary. Twelve runs from five balls then becomes thirteen from the over as he drives to midwicket for a single from the final ball. As we go into the final two overs, the Welsh county are just twenty-four runs away from a stunning triumph.

CAREER BEST

When he reached 18, Michael Kasprowicz recorded a very timely highest score in the premier cup competition, surpassing the 15 he made for Leicestershire against Ireland in Dublin in 1999.

415-7 Darren Thomas 60, Michael Kasprowicz 24　　　　*Hollioake 8-0-68-3*

49TH OVER - ED GIDDINS 8
VAUXHALL END

With runs needed from just about every ball if they are to reach their target, Glamorgan suffer a bad start to the penultimate over as Kasprowicz fails to score from ball one and then can only manage a single from Giddins' second delivery, an excellent yorker. Worse is to follow, however, as the visitors lose their eighth wicket to the next ball. Thomas drives to long-on and calls his partner for a second run but, despite a full-length dive for the crease, the Aussie fast bowler fails to beat a perfect return to the bowler by Adam Hollioake. Glamorgan now require twenty-two runs from nine balls as Andrew Davies arrives at the crease. Thomas is still on strike, of course, but he loses it straight away as he again drives towards long-on and this time takes no chance with Hollioake's arm. Twenty-one from eight deliveries looks nigh on impossible, and, with Davies only able to squeeze the fifth ball of the over, another fine full-length delivery, to backward point for one run, Glamorgan's brave battle seems set to be a losing one. A boundary, preferably a six, is needed from the final ball but the bowler is right on the mark again, allowing Thomas just another single. The penultimate over has cost a mere five runs, Giddins' exceptional last two overs have yielded just twelve and the Welshmen have been left with a mountain to climb - nineteen runs are needed from the final over.

| *420-8 Darren Thomas 63, Andrew Davies 1* | *Giddins 8-0-77-1* |

TJ - Although he had been very harshly treated during his first two spells, I thought Ed Giddins bowled very well during his final two overs, with lots of good blockhole balls. Was that how you saw it?

AB - Yes, he's probably our best bowler at the death. Until Adam came back we didn't really have anyone else who could finish at the end of a game. Ed bowls that yorker length very well whereas we've got a few other bowlers who aren't used to putting it up in the blockhole every ball - and if you don't get it exactly right on a pitch like that one then it can be very costly. He's a banker at the death and he made the last few overs a little easier for us.

TJ - And at the other end we had Adam, who really is the ideal man to have bowling in a tight end-of-innings situation, isn't he?

AB - I'd always back him in that situation and he nearly always comes up trumps. He's got tremendous self-belief as well, which is vital - if you don't believe you can do it then you're in big trouble.

50TH OVER - ADAM HOLLIOAKE 10
PAVILION END

Crucially for Glamorgan's hopes, Darren Thomas starts the last over on strike as Hollioake prepares to bowl. The first ball is driven into the covers but Thomas is unable to get back for a second run, leaving Davies to face the music with eighteen needed from five balls. Under such extreme pressure, the batsman is only able to miscue a lofted drive to wide mid-on where Jimmy Ormond takes a straightforward catch, the only positive thing from a Glamorgan point of view being that the batsmen cross before the catch is completed, putting Thomas back on strike. Victory can only be achieved with a boundary from every ball now, a feat that is surely out of the question. Thomas clearly relishes this challenge, however, immediately smiting Hollioake over the deep backward square leg boundary with a mighty pull for six - twelve runs are now needed from three deliveries and the visitors' faint hopes are still alive. Their prospects brighten still further when Hollioake's next ball strays down the leg-side for a wide - eleven from three - but recede just as quickly when Thomas can only manage one run from the fourth ball after squeezing a full-length delivery away via a mixture of bat and pad. Dean Cosker, no mean tail-ender despite his number eleven position in the order today, is therefore left to face the penultimate delivery with ten runs still required, a clear case of do-or-die. Unfortunately for Glamorgan, Hollioake keeps a cool head and the game ends in spectacular style as Cosker's wild swing fails to make contact with a perfect yorker that removes the off stump. After a pulsating day's cricket, choc-a-block with records and personal bests, Surrey have triumphed by just nine runs with one ball of the plucky visitors' innings unbowled.

429 all out Darren Thomas 71   *Hollioake 8.5-0-77-5*

GLAMORGAN innings								
Fall of wkt	Batsman	How	Out		Score	Balls	4s	6s
2-163	R.D.B. Croft *	c Ward	b Hollioake		119	69	18	3
1-113	I.J. Thomas	run	out		23	19	2	1
6-336	D.L. Hemp	c Ormond	b Bicknell		102	88	10	3
3-197	M.P. Maynard	c Ramprakash	b Giddins		21	19	3	0
4-295	A.Dale	c Clarke	b Hollioake		49	33	6	1
5-295	M.J. Powell	c Giddins	b Hollioake		0	2	0	0
	S.D. Thomas	Not	Out		71	41	5	3
7-352	M.A. Wallace +	c Ramprakash	b Bicknell		5	7	0	0
8-417	M.S. Kasprowicz	run	out		25	18	2	1
9-421	A.P. Davies	c Ormond	b Hollioake		1	2	0	0
10-429	D.A. Cosker		b Hollioake		0	1	0	0
	Extras	(7lb, 6w)			13			
TOTAL	**(49.5 overs)**		**(all out)**		**429**			

Bicknell	10	0	84	2
Giddins	8	0	77	1
Ormond	9	0	72	0
Saqlain Mushtaq	10	0	82	0
Hollioake	8.5	0	77	5
Clarke	4	0	30	0

A clearly disappointed Cosker and Thomas leave the field with a very relieved Surrey team after the most action-packed and frenetic cricket match ever witnessed. The relatively small but totally enthralled and exhausted crowd rises to offer their applause and appreciation for an outstanding day's entertainment as the Surrey players make their way to the changing rooms to exchange handshakes all round with their Glamorgan counterparts. It's a day that will forever be remembered by all those present, be they players or spectators.

TJ - The last over started with Glamorgan needing nineteen to win - surely, by then, you were feeling pretty confident we would win?
AB - I was never 'pretty confident' although I knew after Ed's previous over that it was probably going to take a couple of sixes or some big boundary hitting for them to win it... so every ball that didn't go over the rope was a big bonus for us. I must say it was nice when it was all over and we could walk off having won!
TJ - You were the obvious candidate for the Man Of The Match award, of course, but I guess Adam's contribution in the field - five wickets and two run outs - was almost as important as your innings in the final analysis?
AB - Yeah, not bad! It's fair to say that we probably wouldn't have won it without

him, you're right. It was a day for me to grab the headlines but there were many good performances in the game - like Wardy's and Adam's and also the efforts of several of the Glamorgan guys.

TJ - I assume you were getting plenty of calls from the media for a day or two after the game? County cricket even made it into the sports pages of the tabloids for once!

AB - Well, I'd picked a bad time to achieve the feat, bang in the middle of the World Cup, but, yes, it still got plenty of coverage. I wasn't really too worried about that anyway, it was just nice to perform well and up my career best in the competition by 196!

TJ - I didn't feel that the short boundary was as big a factor as it was made out to be by some people. Would you agree with that?

AB - Yes, I don't think it had a massive effect on the totals. Maybe the scores would have been twenty or thirty lighter but not too many of the sixes just crept over the rope, a lot of them went right out of the ground or at least over most of the seating. The high run tally was mostly down to the very good even-paced wicket where you could actually judge the pace and bounce of the ball quite well and even play front-foot pull shots - which is quite rare and shows how good the pitch was. So, yes, the boundary helped make it a high-scoring game but it didn't ridicule the game - had there been a bigger boundary then I think our 438 might perhaps have become 400-410 but certainly not 360 or anything like that.

TJ - There were a phenomenal number of records broken in this match but I'd guess, from the things you've already said, that records don't worry you a great deal?

AB - I read about all the world records the next day but, no, it's not something that I get too excited about really. All I was really worried about was batting well for Surrey, going past 72 and then getting to a hundred. Once I'd turned it into a big hundred then I started to think about two-hundred and once you've gone past two-hundred then you've really got nothing to lose - if you get out then you've still had a good knock!

TJ - Looking back now, with hindsight, at the way in which Glamorgan won the Norwich Union League title, was this perhaps a better win than many of us realised at the time?

AB - We had a little bit of a score to settle because we felt we should have beaten them in the Benson & Hedges semi-final a couple of years ago but they beat us quite comprehensively in the end. But, yes, I think it was a better win than we gave it credit for at the time - they've proved that they are a top one-day side and their efforts in this game showed what tremendous belief they have.

TJ - Ultimately, of course, the win over Glamorgan counted for nothing in terms of winning the C&G Trophy at the end of the season. Although no-one can take anything away from you for your record-breaking efforts in this match, did the semi-final farce**, and defeat, at Headingley take any of the gloss off your achievement?

** After the first three days set aside for the game were washed out, it was agreed that the match should be played two days later, on the Sunday. With the weather having improved, Yorkshire played a Norwich Union League game the next day (Saturday) on the semi-final pitch and it offered a good deal of encouragement to all the spinners involved in the match. Consequently, on the morning of the re-arranged semi-final, a fresh pitch was cut elsewhere on the damp square, much to the irritation of the umpires, who saw no reason why the original dry pitch should not be used, despite it having been played on the previous day. Yorkshire's actions were reported to the ECB and, at the time of going to press, they look likely to be punished with a two- or three-year ban on playing home ties in the C&G Trophy.

AB - No, not at all. It was a bit disappointing how the goalposts kept moving during the semi-final but that's cricket. I think next year we need to make changes to stop something similar happening again, though. I don't think anyone wanted a bowl-out, we wanted a proper game, so I was in favour of us coming back on the Sunday but I was rather surprised and disappointed to find them 'mowing the lawn' to prepare a new pitch on the morning of the game. I think it's just wrong that a team should be able to play a game on a pitch to see how it's going to pan out and then, if they don't like it, go and move to another pitch. But they played very well in the final to win the trophy so fair play to them there.

TJ - In terms of the most memorable innings and moments of your career where does this performance rank?

AB - It's hard to say but this feat is certainly something that can never be taken away from me. I always thought I could beat 203 - immediately after that innings in 1997 I remember saying that if the wicket was good and the outfield was quick and things go your way then anything could happen - but I'd be very surprised if 268 was beaten in my lifetime.

TJ - To beat 268 everything would have to be perfect for the batsman, wouldn't it?

AB - There are certain grounds where it could be possible - Whitgift is one and Scarborough, Northampton and Taunton are others where high scoring is possible. But, apart from being on one of these grounds and having the right wicket, you also need everything to go your way - you need a bit of luck, as I had on this day when I was dropped on 47. You've also got to play positively right from the start and maintain it for fifty overs and you've almost certainly got to open the batting. So apart from that it's straightforward - good luck!

TJ - I suppose the only disappointing thing to come out of the day was that no benefit collection had been scheduled for you?!

AB - Had we known that all the rest of our ties in the competition were going to be away from home then we probably would have done one but we had one shortly afterwards and people's memories were long enough for them to make very generous donations later in the season anyway. But a benefit season can be very tiring and stressful so I'm just pleased to have come out of it with a world record, half-a-dozen centuries and over two-thousand runs to my credit in all competitions

COMPLETE MATCH SCORECARD

SURREY v GLAMORGAN at THE AMP OVAL. Played on 19th June 2002

Surrey won the toss
Umpires:- I.J. Gould & P. Wil

SURREY				Balls	4s	6s		O	M	R	W
1- 286	I.J. Ward		b Croft	97	95	8	4	Kasprowicz	10	0	53	1
5- 431	A.D. Brown		b Kasprowicz	268	160	30	12	Davies	8	0	88	0
2- 354	M.R. Ramprakash		c & b S.D. Thomas	26	27	2	0	S.D. Thomas	9	0	108	3
3- 376	R.R. Clarke	c Wallace	b S.D. Thomas	5	6	0	0	Croft	8	0	62	1
4- 424	A.J. Hollioake *	c I.J. Thomas	b S.D. Thomas	4	6	0	0	Dale	8	0	68	0
	A.J. Stewart	Not Out		2	4	0	0	Cosker	7	0	51	0
	J.N. Batty +	Not Out		6	3	1	0					
	M.P. Bicknell	did not bat										
	Saqlain Mushtaq	did not bat										
	J. Ormond	did not bat										
	E.S.H. Giddins	did not bat										
	Extras (8lb, 20w, 2nb)			30								
	TOTAL		(50 overs)	**438 - 5**								

GLAMORGAN				Balls	4s	6s		O	M	R	W
2- 162	R.D.B. Croft *	c Ward	b Hollioake	119	69	18	3	Bicknell	10	0	84	2
1- 113	I.J. Thomas	run out		23	19	2	1	Giddins	8	0	77	1
6- 336	D.L. Hemp	c Ormond	b Bicknell	102	88	10	3	Ormond	9	0	72	0
3- 197	M.P. Maynard	c Ramprakash	b Giddins	21	19	3	0	Saqlain	10	0	82	0
4- 295	A. Dale	c Clarke	b Hollioake	49	33	6	1	Hollioake	8 .5	0	77	5
5- 295	M.J. Powell	c Giddins	b Hollioake	0	2	0	0	Clarke	4	0	30	0
	S.D. Thomas	Not Out		71	41	5	3					
7- 352	M.A. Wallace +	c Ramprakash	b Bicknell	5	7	0	0					
8- 417	M.S. Kasprowicz	run out		25	18	2	1					
9- 421	A.P. Davies	c Ormond	b Hollioake	1	2	0	0					
10- 429	D.A. Cosker		b Hollioake	0	1	0	0					
	Extras (7lb, 6w)			13								
	TOTAL		(49.5 overs)	**429**								

SURREY WON BY NINE RUNS

45

ALI BROWN'S WORLD RECORD-BREAKING 268
Original run chart as compiled by Mark Smith

A.D. Brown   268 Runs   (200 Minutes)

C&G Trophy – 4th Round	Bowler	Balls	Runs	4s	6s	Partnership		R	B	M
Surrey v Glamorgan	M.S. Kasprowicz	17	17	3	-	Ward	(97:171)	286	211	142
AMP Oval - 19th June 2002	A.P. Davies	34	71	12	2	Rampk'sh	(26:33)	68	48	27
	S.D. Thomas	33	73	6	6	Clarke	(5:14)	22	12	9
50 46m 38b 7X4 2X6	R.D.B. Croft	27	43	2	4	Hollioake	(4:44)	48	19	13
100 99m 80b 10X4 4X6	A. Dale	29	51	7	-	Stewart	(1:6)	7	6	5
150 127m 104b 16X4 7X6	D.A. Cosker	20	13	-	-					
200 165m 134b 20X4 10X6	TOTAL	160	268	30	12					
250 191m 153b 26X4 12X6										

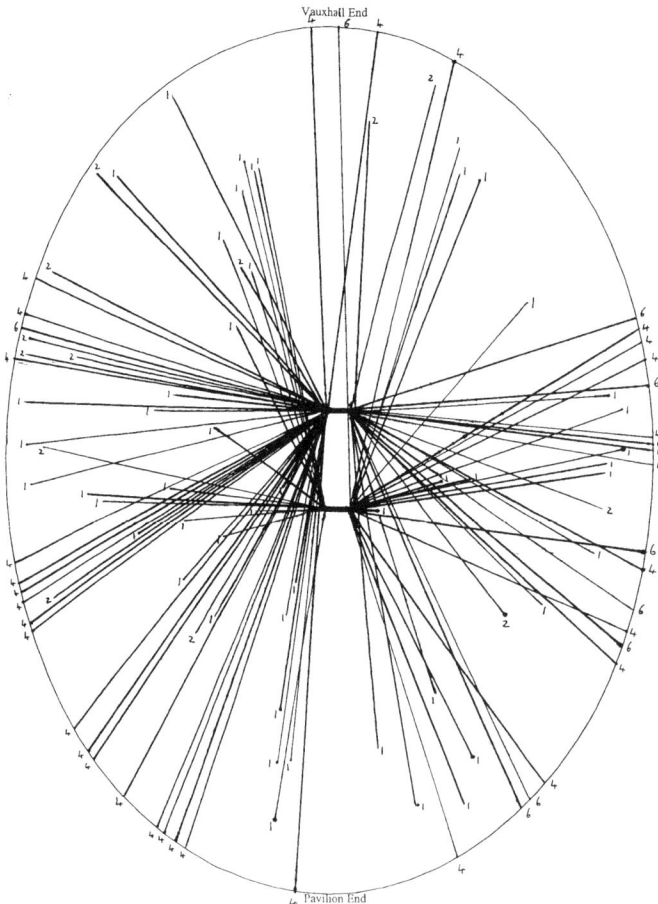

46

4 WHAT THE PLAYERS SAID...

...ABOUT THE MATCH

Robert Croft, Glamorgan's stand-in captain

'It was disappointing to lose but I'm very proud of every one of those players in the dressing room. We were staring down the barrel of a rather large gun at half-time but we really gave it a go and played for the badge on the shirt.'

'There wasn't actually a heck of a lot of pressure facing a total like that. I just said to the boys before going out there, plain and simple, "Smash it!"'

'I'm not a cricketer who wants to lose by 100 runs - I'd rather lose by 300 runs having given it a go. It was a great game of cricket and the spirit we have shown to take the game into the final over was amazing.'

'Of course, it's disappointing to lose and everyone in the dressing room is down. But if we play like that then we will win a lot of games this season. I hope this is not only the making of our season - but for the next three or four years to come. I've got the utmost respect for youngsters like Ian Thomas and they will benefit from that.'

'It's disappointing to come to a Test ground and have a 55-yard boundary but it was the same for both sides and I don't understand if the public don't want to come and watch matches like that.'

'It was a great pitch to play on; a flat one that helps improve the technique of batsmen and encourages bowlers to develop and make sure they put the ball in the right place. We need more of these pitches in English cricket.'

'I told the boys to show passion and pride and we did that. I think we gave a performance that both ourselves as a team and the whole nation can be proud of.'

Darren Thomas

'The game was a freak show and every bowler took stick. I bowled a few bad balls and Alistair Brown came off, but I also took three wickets and ended up with an average of 36. But it was a day when every bowler was punished. Saqlain Mushtaq is a world-class bowler but he conceded 82 from ten overs. I was a bit down when I got home and was told my name had been on the radio. The last thing you want to hear after a drilling is that you're in some record book for conceding runs but, to be honest, I'm not bothered. I think it's pretty sad that people are. It's a blow for me but I'll just look to the next game and try to get over that hurdle when it comes.'

Darren Thomas (continued)

'We were lucky to have enough balls (to complete the match). One seemed to be coming back from outside the ground just as another was going out of it. But at least we let them know they were in a game - Browny said afterwards that the fifty overs he spent in the field were the most frightening of his life. He just didn't expect to lose after spending the best fifty overs of his career at the crease.'

John Derrick, Glamorgan coach

'We had a bit of laugh at halfway when we saw some of the bowling figures. You don't think 440 is gettable but we had a good start and thought, "Hang on a minute". The attitude was fantastic and that shows the sort of team spirit we have.'

Ed Giddins

'It was a freak of a game. It was absolutely incredible - it will never happen again. I woke up this morning and had to pinch myself that it was real, that it hadn't just been a dream. It wasn't as if conditions were unusual - we've all played on flat wickets with a short boundary before. We thought that the Glamorgan batsmen would nick one or hit it up in the air, but they didn't. Robert Croft played like Bradman.'

Martin Bicknell

'We were under the impression that the second half of the game would be nothing more than a stroll in the park. At 20-0 after five deliveries of the first over of Glamorgan's reply, bowled by yours truly, worrying thoughts started creeping into our heads. What followed will never be forgotten. Full credit must go to Glamorgan and it just shows what can be achieved.'

Ali Brown

'I was very nervous towards the end of the Glamorgan innings. I didn't think they would get anywhere near our total, but they went all the way. Every time the game looked dead they came back. And when Darren Thomas hit a six over my head in the last over I began to get worried.'

Keith Medlycott, Surrey cricket manager

'Glamorgan deserve a lot of credit for the way they came out and competed when all seemed lost.'

Angus Fraser, former Middlesex and England seamer

'It was a fantastic effort by Glamorgan. You could see it slipping away in the field but to turn it around and put up such a strong batting performance is a wonderful effort.'

TOP: Ali Brown drives elegantly through extra cover... *(Peter Frost)*
BOTTOM: ...but it's all over for Ian Ward as Robert Croft manages to sneak a ball through his defences *(Phil Walter - Empics)*

i

TOP: Can we have our ball back, please? Yes, I know it's the fifth time...
BOTTOM: 'Sorry, Crofty, but that's another six'. Umpire Peter Willey is starting
to look a little weary as he raises his arms to signal another 'maximum'
(Peter Frost)

TOP: Brown crashes the ball through the off-side again
BOTTOM: Having just reached his double-century, Brown raises his bat to the crowd while
the battered bowler, Andrew Davies, looks ready to wave the white flag
(Phil Walter - Empics)

TOP: Take that! Another mighty leg-side blow sends the ball flying to the boundary.
BOTTOM: The end of the road. Kasprowicz's yorker finally brings Brown's
epic innings to a dramatic close.
(Peter Frost)

History made, and with a trail of broken records behind him, Ali Brown leaves the field to a well-deserved standing ovation

(Phil Walter - Empics)

TOP: Robert Croft lauches the ball down the ground... *(Peter Frost)*
BOTTOM: ...and celebrates as he completes his superb century *(Phil Walter - Empics)*

An exhausted and relieved Surrey team heads back to the dressing room after completing their nine-run win

(Phil Walter - Empics)

TOP: The bat that did the damage. At the Club awards evening with Alan Copping, Sponsorship Manager of AMP, and Mike Soper, Surrey Chairman
(Adam Davy - Empics)
BOTTOM: Brown receives an engraved salver from his club side to commemorate his achievement. David Morgan of Cheam Cricket Club applauds while, ominously for future generations of bowlers, Ali's son, Max, tries on some batting gloves for size.
(Joan Elgar)

...ABOUT ALI BROWN'S INNINGS

Robert Croft, Glamorgan's stand-in captain
'The way that Ali Brown struck the ball today is something I guarantee you that the people who were here today will never see again. It was such clean striking and I'm pleased it took something pretty special to beat my side. It was phenomenal. We had some early chances but didn't take them.'

Darren Thomas
'It was absolute carnage and I don't expect to experience it again - at least I hope I don't. I must take my hat off to Browny. It was a magnificent innings although we dropped him very early on. He was in the zone but he did play intelligently. He seemed to start every over I bowled to him by hitting the first ball through extra cover; then, when I dragged my length back, he would go back and play a pull or pick-up shot to the short leg-side boundary. He was piercing the field every ball, whereas I reckon we found Ramps, who was sweeping on that short boundary, about twenty to thirty times. Browny must have beaten our sweeper on ten to fifteen occasions.'

Martin Bicknell
'As you may know, I have always thought of Browny as nothing more than a slogger, but 268 certainly takes some slogging! To witness his innings was very special.'

Ali Brown
'It's 268 runs more than I scored in the previous round against Scotland! I had butterflies before the start, which with me is a good sign. I've been in good form recently, my feet are right, my weight is right. I'm probably in the best form of my life.'

'It's hard to compare knocks, particularly from a few years ago, but I think this one is my best-ever one-day knock. To get a big score like that everything has to go right. You need a good pitch and a shortish boundary and the odd bit of luck along the way. I'd be surprised if anyone beats 268. He'll have to bat pretty well.'

Keith Medlycott, Surrey cricket manager
'Never before in my cricket career have I seen anyone bat as emphatically as Ali Brown did today.'

Angus Fraser, former Middlesex and England seamer
'It's unbelievable. It is a magnificent effort by him - I'm just pleased I was not bowling.'

5 WHAT THE PRESS SAID...

...ABOUT THE MATCH

'...a bizarre match that might easily have been directed by Luis Bunuel and scripted by Chuck Jones... the least bowler-friendly contest in the 40-year history of the abbreviated game...'
Rob Steen, The Guardian

'It was one-day cricket at its very, very best.'
Lawrence Booth, Daily Telegraph

'An extraordinary match crammed with staggering batting feats, a welter of statistical landmarks and a world-record aggregate score in the one-day game...'
David Llewellyn, The Independent

'All day... boundaries flowed like water, records fell like autumn leaves and between them Surrey, the victors, and Glamorgan, the truly gallant losers, scored 867 runs in 99 overs and five balls.'
Christopher Martin-Jenkins, The Times

'...the most extraordinary limited-overs game ever played.'
Brian Scovell, Daily Mail

'On a day when the likes of Alistair Brown, Robert Croft and David Hemp were in danger of disturbing local air traffic, let alone the London buses that skirt The Oval, 87 fours and 28 sixes were struck as records tumbled by the score.'
Phil Blanche, The Western Mail

...ABOUT ALI BROWN'S INNINGS

'Brown, whose modest physique belies the power of England's most exhilarating batsman since Ian Botham, scored his runs off 160 balls, leaving Graeme Pollock's 222 not out... whimpering in the distance.'
Rob Steen, The Guardian

'...a Bradmanesque mixture of poetry and murder.'
Lawrence Booth, Daily Telegraph

'Brown's innings was a display of savage grace, fashioned through a combination of brutal power and beautiful timing.'
David Llewellyn, The Independent

'...a phenomenal piece of cultured hitting...'
Christopher Martin-Jenkins, The Times

'Brown's strokeplay was peerless and he hit the ball even harder than Ian Botham or Sir Viv Richards.'
Brian Scovell, Daily Mail

'The day belonged to Brown. There are few, if any, more destructive players in the county game and his absence from England one-day squads proves that curious selection policy affects even the elite.'
Phil Blanche, The Western Mail

6 VIEWS FROM THE SURREY DRESSING ROOM

At the end of the season I asked some of Ali Brown's colleagues to answer the following six questions about that incredible day in June. Their answers are given below.

1) Please give me three words to describe Browny's 268...
2) ... and three words to describe the match
3) Can you honestly see the record of 268 ever being beaten?
4) How much of Browny's knock did you actually see?
5) At what stage did you realise that something very special was taking place out in the middle?
6) Was there any point when you genuinely felt that Glamorgan would win the match?

MARK RAMPRAKASH

1) Awesome, Controlled, Power
2) Breathtaking, Draining, Entertaining
3) No, certainly not against a first-class county anyway
4) Pretty much the whole lot - I was next man in!
5) It's hard to say because he reached his hundred pretty quickly and he never really changed his momentum very much. The pace of his innings remained pretty much the same, he never resorted to slogging or being reckless - it was a very controlled knock
6) Yes, Thomas was going well and then Kasprowicz hit a long ball, so at that point I thought it was very much in the balance.

ALEC STEWART

1) Just Awesome Batting
2) Incredible Amazing Match
3) I played in the game where Lara scored 375 to break the Test record. Probably when Sobers scored his 366 people said it would never be beaten but... never say never. 268 is an unbelievable score and if it is ever beaten then it will be incredible and it would be a great innings to see.
4) I always watch so I'd say I saw all of it... well, certainly 99.9%. I was at the other end when he got out so everyone is going to forget my innings of 2 not out!
5) Well, he knocked up his hundred in such quick time that it was always possible that something special could happen... with Browny, anything is possible, that's the thing.
6) The way Croft set off at the start and then the way Hemp and Thomas batted later on they got themselves into a great position to knock the runs off and win the game. Normally, defending 438 the game is won, so long as you go about things the right way, but we soon felt that we might just have a game on our hands. It was a little strange for me because I wasn't keeping wicket that day - normally I'd

be right in the thick of things but as I was fielding at long off and third man I was kind of looking at it from afar. It was a bit disconcerting to be stood there with the ball disappearing over my head and to the boundary every second or third ball. I kept looking at the scoreboard and thinking 'is 438 really safe?' but in the end you just have to back yourself to pull through and win.

ADAM HOLLIOAKE
1) Freakish, Awesome, Unbelievable.
2) Same as above!
3) So long as Alistair Brown is playing then I think it can be beaten, yes!
4) I watched every single ball.
5) I think when the opening partnership started approaching 200, and then it grew from there - I remember the boys walking around the changing room saying 'What the hell is going on here'.
6) Yes, I remember walking past Rikki Clarke at one point and saying 'What is going on, we're losing here'! I think there were a couple of stages when I was very concerned - I recall one of them being just before I took two wickets in three balls. But the game just wouldn't die, even in the last over. I was thinking that if we lost we'd be going into the record books for all the wrong reasons so it was a big relief when we finally won it.

RIKKI CLARKE
1) Unbelievable, Classy, Powerful.
2) Unbelievable, Freakish, Crazy.
3) No, I can't see it happening, not in an innings of 50 overs anyway. I doubt that I'll ever witness anything quite like that again in my career.
4) I went to get some treatment from the physio at one point but, otherwise, I saw all of it.
5) When Browny got to about 150 you just knew that he was going to go for something big - he always sets himself targets to get big scores. I can't exactly pinpoint the moment when I realised something very special was happening but I was just pleased to be there to witness such an incredible innings.
6) When they came out with a lot of shots early on I thought 'good on them for having a go but they won't get anywhere near the total' but by the time we reached the last five overs I was getting a bit panicky. I remember thinking that if we lost the match it would have been a hell of a game of cricket... but I wouldn't understand how we could have been beaten with 438 on the board.

MARTIN BICKNELL
1) Awesome, Destructive, Powerful.
2) Nightmare, Astounding, Unbelievable.
3) No, I really can't. Maybe it's ridiculous to say 'never' but you'd need so much going for you to beat that score. It's next to impossible.

4) Most of it. And it was just incredible.

5) At one stage when he was on about 160, I really thought there was a chance he could go on and make 300 if he kept hammering away... and he didn't end up too far short. He was going berserk and kept nailing every shot. We kept looking at one another and saying 'he's just hit another extraordinary shot and hit another six'. And it just kept happening.

6) Yes, I have to say there were times when I thought we were going to lose. I felt there was a real chance of them winning when it got down to the last ten overs but, saying that, you kept thinking that something was going to happen in a minute - we were going to get a couple of wickets or they were going to have a bad over... but they just didn't. They just kept coming at us and the game never died, that was the thing. Incredible.

JON BATTY

1) I'm struggling to find words that are worthy. There are no words to describe it, really... indescribable.

2) Freakish, exhilarating, unforgettable.

3) No... never.

4) Pretty much all of it. If I'm batting at seven then I like to try and get away from watching the game for about half an hour at the start, to relax a little bit, but the way we were going I couldn't tear myself away from it on this occasion.

5) It was incredible right from the start really... I think there was a period when we'd been batting for twenty overs or so when we thought we could get three-hundred then, about twenty minutes later, someone said 'I think we can get 350' then, half-an-hour after that, somebody said 'I reckon we'll get up to 400'. It was ridiculous how our view of our possible total kept changing.

6) There was no point that I thought we would lose the game up until there were five overs to go. Even then I wasn't expecting us to lose but that was the first time when I thought 'hang on a minute, this could get very tight'... and it did. I always felt that one tight over, going for just a couple of runs, would blow them completely out of the water but it just never happened.

6 STATISTICAL COMPENDIUM

WHERE ALI BROWN'S 268 RUNS WERE SCORED

RUNS SCORED	1s	2s	3s	4s	6s	Total Runs
Through mid-off	9	0	0	3	1	27
Other strokes in front of square - off-side	14	4	0	17	1	96
Behind Square - off-side	6	4	0	6	1	44
TOTAL - OFF-SIDE	**29**	**8**	**0**	**26**	**3**	**167**
Through mid-on	8	0	0	0	3	26
Other strokes in front of square - leg-side	8	3	0	2	5	52
Behind Square - leg-side	5	2	0	2	1	23
TOTAL - LEG-SIDE	**21**	**5**	**0**	**4**	**9**	**101**
GRAND TOTAL	**50**	**13**	**0**	**30**	**12**	**268**

ALI BROWN'S FIFTY-RUN MILESTONES

Ov	Milestone	Balls	6s	4s		Balls	6s	4s
1	Takes guard	0	0	0				
12	Reaches 50	38	2	7	Stats for first 50	38	2	7
25	Reaches 100	80	4	10	Stats for second 50	42	2	3
32	Reaches 150	104	7	16	Stats for third 50	24	3	6
42	Reaches 200	134	10	20	Stats for fourth 50	30	3	4
48	Reaches 250	153	12	26	Stats for fifth 50	19	2	6
50	Out for 268	160	12	30	Stats for final 18	7	0	4

THE TEN HIGHEST INDIVIDUAL INNINGS RECORDED IN FIRST-CLASS LIMITED-OVERS CRICKET

Score	Batsman	For	Against	Venue	Year
268	A.D. BROWN	SURREY	GLAMORGAN	AMP OVAL	2002
222*	R.G. Pollock	Eastern Province	Border	East London	1974/75
206	A.I. Kallicharran	Warwickshire	Oxfordshire	Edgbaston	1984
203	A.D. Brown	Surrey	Hampshire	Guildford	1997
202*	A. Barrow	Natal	S.A. African XI	Durban	1975/76
201	V.J. Wells	Leicestershire	Berkshire	Leicester	1996
198*	G.A. Gooch	Essex	Sussex	Hove	1982
197*	Sajid Ali	National Bank	United Bank	Karachi	1996/97
194	Saeed Anwar	Pakistan	India	Madras	1996/97
191	D.S. Lehmann	Yorkshire	Nottinghamshire	Scarborough	2001

MATCH MANHATTANS

SURREY INNINGS (438-5)

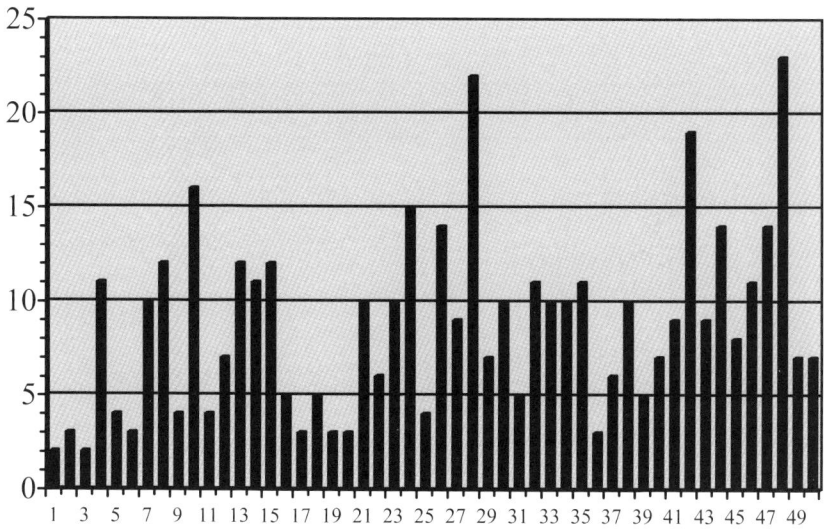

GLAMORGAN INNINGS (429)

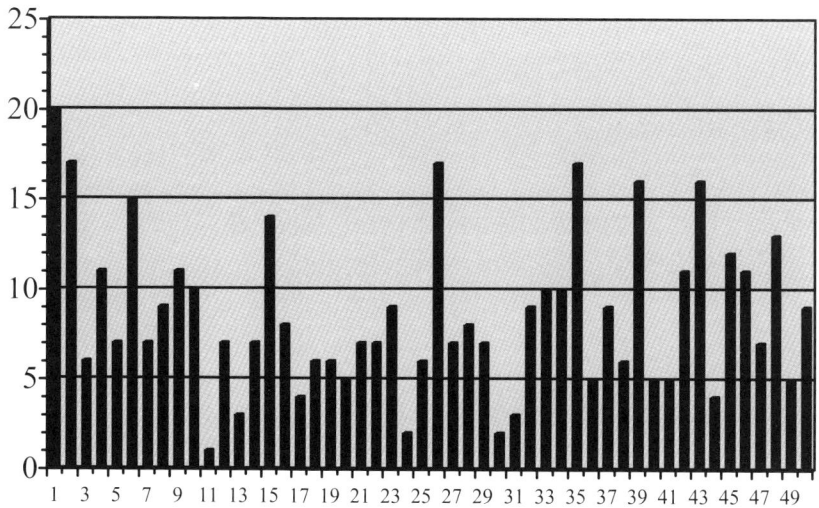

END-OF-OVER SCORES GRAPH

HOW GLAMORGAN LED THE WAY FOR MOST OF THE MATCH

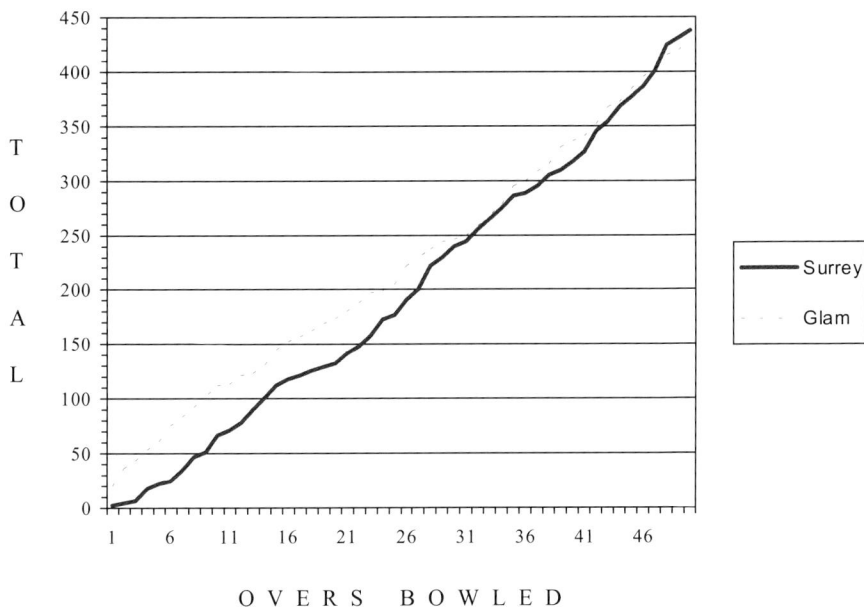

OVERS BOWLED

HIGHEST TEAM SCORES RECORDED
IN FIRST-CLASS LIMITED-OVERS CRICKET

Score	Overs	By	Against	Venue	Season
438-5	50	Surrey	Glamorgan	AMP Oval	2002
429	49.5	Glamorgan	Surrey	AMP Oval	2002
424-5*	50	Buckinghamshire	Suffolk	Dinton	2002
413-4	60	Somerset	Devon	Torquay	1990
409-6	50	Trinidad	Northern Windwards	Kingston	2001/02
406-5	60	Leicestershire	Berkshire	Leicester	1996
404-3	60	Worcestershire	Devon	Worcester	1987
398-5	50	Sri Lanka	Kenya	Kandy	1995/96
397-4	50	New South Wales	Tasmania	Sydney	2001/02
392-6	50	India	India B	Chennai	2000/01
392-5	60	Warwickshire	Oxfordshire	Edgbaston	1984

* This total was scored on 29th August, some nine weeks after Surrey set the world record

ALI BROWN's WORLD RECORD-BREAKING 268 CONDENSED

Ball	Bowler	Outcome	Runs	Score
1	MK	Thick edge/steer to third man	1	1
2	ADs	No run	.	1
3	ADs	Miscued hook backward of square leg	2	3
4	ADs	No run	.	3
5	ADs	No run	.	3
6	ADs	No run	.	3
7	ADs	No run	.	3
8	ADs	Driven through extra cover	4	7
9	ADs	Driven backward of point	2	9
10	ADs	Pulled wide of mid-on	4	13
11	ADs	No run	.	13
12	ADs	Sliced drive to third man	1	14
13	MK	No run	.	14
14	MK	No run	.	14
15	MK	No run	.	14
16	MK	No run	.	14
17	MK	No run	.	14
18	MK	Lofted drive over cover	4	18
19	ADs	No run	.	18
20	ADs	No run	.	18
21	ADs	No run	.	18
22	ADs	No run	.	18
23	MK	Glanced to long leg	1	19
24	ADs	Lofted drive over extra cover	4	23
25	ADs	Driven through covers	4	27
26	ADs	No run	.	27
27	ADs	No run	.	27
28	ADs	No run	.	27
29	ADs	Squeezed into the ground and past wicketkeeper	4	31
30	MK	Leg bye	.	31
31	DT	No run	.	31
32	DT	Pulled over midwicket	6	37
33	DT	Lofted drive over extra cover	4	41
34	DT	Lofted drive over wide mid-on	6	47
35	DT	No run	.	47
36	DT	No run	.	47
37	DT	Dropped chance - edged slash high to right of wicketkeeper	2	49
38	DT	Sliced drive to third man	1	50
39	DT	No run	.	50
40	ADs	Driven through covers	4	54
41	ADs	Driven wide of mid-on	1	55
42	DT	No run	.	55
43	DT	Lofted drive over square cover	6	61
44	DT	No run	.	61
45	DT	Driven to deep square cover	1	62
46	RC	Clipped backward of square leg	1	63
47	RC	Lofted straight drive	6	69
48	RC	No run	.	69

Ball	Bowler	Outcome	Runs	Score
49	RC	No run	.	69
50	RC	Cut backward of point	4	73
51	ADl	No run	.	73
52	ADl	Clipped through midwicket	2	75
53	ADl	Cut through point	2	77
54	ADl	No run	.	77
55	ADl	No run	.	77
56	RC	Driven to long-on	1	78
57	RC	No run	.	78
58	ADl	Forced to deep mid-off	1	79
59	ADl	Glanced to fine leg	2	81
60	RC	Whipped through square leg	1	82
61	RC	No run	.	82
62	RC	No run	.	82
63	ADl	Forced straight down the ground	1	83
64	RC	Whipped backward of square leg	1	84
65	RC	Clipped backward of square leg	1	85
66	ADl	Forced into the covers	1	86
67	ADl	Driven wide of mid-on	2	88
68	ADl	Whipped through square leg	1	89
69	DC	Pushed backward of point	1	90
70	DC	No run	.	90
71	DC	Driven to deep extra cover	1	91
72	ADl	No run	.	91
73	ADl	Driven through extra cover	4	95
74	ADl	Cut backward of point	2	97
75	ADl	Forced into the covers	1	98
76	DC	No run	.	98
77	DC	No run	.	98
78	DC	Lofted towards long-on	1	99
79	DC	No run	.	99
80	DC	Pushed to cover	1	100
81	DT	Driven to long-off	1	101
82	DT	No run	.	101
83	DT	Driven through extra cover	4	105
84	DT	Pulled high over midwicket and out of the ground	6	111
85	DT	Pushed to square cover	1	112
86	DC	Driven wide of mid-on	1	113
87	DC	No run	.	113
88	DC	Pushed backward of square leg	1	114
89	DT	Driven to deep square cover	1	115
90	DT	Sliced drive over point	4	119
91	DT	Pulled high over backward square leg and out of the ground	6	125
92	DT	Lofted drive over extra cover	4	129
93	MK	No run	.	129
94	MK	Driven to deep cover	1	130
95	ADl	Cut through point	4	134
96	ADl	No run	.	134
97	ADl	Lofted drive wide of long-off	4	138
98	ADl	No run	.	138
99	ADl	Cut to deep square cover	1	139

Ball	Bowler	Outcome	Runs	Score
100	MK	No run	.	139
101	MK	Steered backward of point	4	143
102	MK	Driven to deep square cover	1	144
103	RC	No run	.	144
104	RC	Pull-driven over wide long-on	6	150
105	RC	Swept backward of square leg	4	154
106	RC	No run	.	154
107	RC	No run	.	154
108	RC	Driven to long-on	1	155
109	MK	Cut to deep square cover	1	156
110	MK	Lofted drive over mid-off	4	160
111	RC	Slog-swept high over midwicket and out of the ground	6	166
112	RC	Driven to long-off	1	167
113	RC	Driven to long-off	1	168
114	DC	Clipped through midwicket	2	170
115	DC	Driven to long-on	1	171
116	DC	No run	.	171
117	RC	No run	.	171
118	RC	Driven to deep midwicket	1	172
119	DC	Driven to long-on	1	173
120	DC	Driven to long-off	1	174
121	RC	Lofted drive high into Lock Stand upper tier at wide long-on	6	180
122	RC	Driven to long-on	1	181
123	RC	No run	.	181
124	RC	Driven wide of mid-on	1	182
125	DC	Two leg-byes	.	182
126	DC	Leg-bye	.	182
127	ADs	Driven to long-off	1	183
128	DC	Lofted drive down to long-off	1	184
129	DC	Driven to long-on	1	185
130	ADs	Driven backward of point	2	187
131	ADs	Lofted drive backward of point	2	189
132	ADs	Driven through extra cover	4	193
133	ADs	Pulled over midwicket	6	199
134	ADs	Lofted drive over extra cover	4	203
135	DT	No run	.	203
136	DT	No-ball, beamer, evaded but not scored off	.	203
137	DT	Clipped through square leg	1	204
138	ADl	Cut to deep point	1	205
139	ADl	Driven through extra cover	4	209
140	ADl	Cut through square cover	2	211
141	ADl	Driven through extra cover	2	213
142	ADl	Lofted drive over extra cover	4	217
143	DT	Forced to long-off	1	218
144	ADl	Lofted drive over extra cover	4	222
145	ADl	Driven to deep cover	1	223
146	ADl	Lofted straight drive	4	227
147	ADl	Driven to long-off	1	228
148	DT	Driven through cover	4	232
149	DT	Upper cut backward of point	6	238
150	DT	Clipped through midwicket	1	239

Ball	Bowler	Outcome	Runs	Score
151	DT	Cut to deep point	1	240
152	ADs	Lofted drive over extra cover	4	244
153	ADs	Pulled high over wide long-on	6	250
154	ADs	Cut backward of point	4	254
155	ADs	Shuffled across stumps and flicked down to fine leg	4	258
156	ADs	Driven wide of mid-on	4	262
157	DT	Cut backward of point	4	266
158	DT	Late cut to third man	1	267
159	DT	Miscued square cut to backward point	1	268
160	MK	OUT, stepping to off side, defeated by yorker-length delivery	.	268

ROBERT CROFT's WHIRLWIND 119 CONDENSED

Ball	Bowler	Outcome	Runs	Score
1	MB	Driven over backward point	4	4
2	MB	Driven wide of mid-on	4	8
3	MB	Forced through extra cover	4	12
4	MB	Driven over mid-off	4	16
5	MB	Sliced drive backward of point	4	20
6	MB	No run	.	20
7	EG	Lofted straight drive	4	24
8	EG	Driven through extra cover	4	28
9	EG	No run	.	28
10	MB	Whipped through midwicket	4	32
11	MB	No run	.	32
12	MB	Skied into space on off-side	1	33
13	EG	Sliced drive backward of point	4	37
14	EG	Driven through extra cover	4	41
15	EG	No run	.	41
16	EG	No run	.	41
17	EG	Forced to mid-off	1	42
18	MB	Lofted straight drive	4	46
19	MB	No run	.	46
20	MB	Driven to mid-off	1	47
21	MB	Driven to mid-off	1	48
22	JO	Pulled over wide long-on	6	54
23	JO	Miscued into leg-side gap	1	55
24	MB	Smashed wide of mid-on	4	59
25	MB	Driven to mid-on	1	60
26	MB	Forced to long-off	1	61
27	JO	No run	.	61
28	JO	Pulled over midwicket	6	67
29	JO	Cut backward of point	2	69
30	JO	No run	.	69
31	JO	Forced to mid-off - no run, but poor throw leads to overthrow	1	70
32	SM	No run	.	70
33	SM	Lofted drive over long-off	6	76
34	SM	Cut backward of point	2	78
35	SM	Pushed into space at midwicket	2	80
36	SM	No run	.	80
37	SM	Pushed to point	1	81

Ball	Bowler	Outcome	Runs	Score
38	JO	Driven through square cover	4	85
39	JO	No run	.	85
40	JO	Pulled over mid-on	4	89
41	JO	No run	.	89
42	JO	Squeezed full-length delivery down to third man	1	90
43	SM	No run	.	90
44	SM	No run	.	90
45	SM	Driven to mid-on	1	91
46	JO	No run	.	91
47	JO	No run	.	91
48	JO	No run	.	91
49	JO	Edged to third man	4	95
50	JO	Pushed to cover	1	96
51	SM	No run	.	96
52	SM	No run	.	96
53	SM	No run	.	96
54	SM	Clipped over midwicket	2	98
55	JO	Driven to mid-off	1	99
56	JO	Steered to third man	1	100
57	SM	No run	.	100
58	SM	Lofted drive wide of mid-on	4	104
59	SM	Lofted straight drive	4	108
60	SM	Miscued drive backward of square leg	1	109
61	AH	Clipped to deep midwicket	1	110
62	AH	Forced to long-off	4	114
63	AH	Driven to deep cover	1	115
64	JO	Top edged hook to long leg - chance, but Giddins slow to react	1	116
65	JO	No run	.	116
66	JO	Driven to deep cover	1	117
67	AH	No run	.	117
68	AH	Lofted into leg-side space	2	119
69	AH	OUT to skier into the covers	.	119

BOWLERS ROLL OF HONOUR
THE OVERS THAT ESCAPED SERIOUS PUNISHMENT

1 RUN CONCEDED (two instances)
Saqlain Mushtaq
11th over of Glamorgan's innings to Ian Thomas (1 ball), Croft (3 balls) and Hemp (2 balls)
Ed Giddins
24th over of Glamorgan's innings to Maynard (3), Dale (2) and Hemp (1)

2 RUNS CONCEDED (four instances)
Michael Kasprowicz
1st over of Surrey's innings to Ward (5) and Brown (1)
Michael Kasprowicz
3rd over of Surrey's innings to Ward (6)
Dean Cosker
39th over of Surrey's innings to Ramprakash (4) and Brown (2)
Rikki Clarke
30th over of Glamorgan's innings to Hemp (5) and Dale (1)

3 RUNS CONCEDED (ten instances)
Andrew Davies
2nd over of Surrey's innings to Brown (6)
Andrew Davies
6th over of Surrey's innings to Ward (2) and Brown (6)
Michael Kasprowicz
9th over of Surrey's innings to Ward (5) and Brown (1)
Robert Croft
17th over of Surrey's innings to Ward (4) and Brown (2)
Robert Croft
19th over of Surrey's innings to Ward (3) and Brown (3)
Adrian Dale
20th over of Surrey's innings to Ward (5) and Brown (1)
Robert Croft
36th over of Surrey's innings to Ward (1), Ramprakash (3) and Brown (2)
Saqlain Mushtaq
13th over of Glamorgan's innings to Hemp (2) and Croft (4)
Martin Bicknell
31st over of Glamorgan's innings to Dale (3) and Hemp (3)
Adam Hollioake
36th over of Glamorgan's innings to Dale (1), Powell (2), Darren Thomas (1) and Hemp (2)

NOTE - These 'runs conceded' totals only include runs off the bat plus no-balls and wides. Leg-byes and byes do not count towards bowlers' analyses.

ANALYSIS OF BOUNDARY HITS DURING THE MATCH

For the purposes of this analysis, the short-side boundary, assuming a right-handed batsman taking guard at the pavilion end, covers the arc from wide long-off round to third man - the straight-hitting boundaries were of conventional length. Surrey appear to have utilised the shorter boundary better than Glamorgan, though it is interesting to note that a sizeable majority of the overall boundary hits found the rope in other areas of the ground.

ALI BROWN ONLY	To the short-side boundary		To all other parts of ground	
Bowling From	6s	4s	6s	4s
PAVILION END	7	4	3	19
VAUXHALL END	1	7	1	0
TOTAL	8	11	4	19

ALL SURREY BATSMEN	To the short-side boundary		To all other parts of ground	
Bowling From	6s	4s	6s	4s
PAVILION END	7	7	3	20
VAUXHALL END	5	11	1	3
TOTAL	12	18	4	23

ALL GLAMORGAN BATSMEN	To the short-side boundary		To all other parts of ground	
Bowling From	6s	4s	6s	4s
PAVILION END	5	4	2	16
VAUXHALL END	3	6	2	20
TOTAL	8	10	4	36

ALL BATSMEN BOTH TEAMS	To the short-side boundary		To all other parts of ground	
Bowling From	6s	4s	6s	4s
PAVILION END	12	11	5	36
VAUXHALL END	8	17	3	23
TOTAL	20	28	8	59

8 SUMMARY OF BROKEN RECORDS

Trying to track down all the records that were broken during this incredible match was quite a task so I suspect there are one or two that I've missed along the way. Although I still believe this to be the most definitive list of records so far produced, I offer my apologies in advance for any omissions! More difficult still was the job of ascertaining what the previous best mark had been in the case of the 'most boundaries in an innings' records. Unfortunately, limited-overs records are less diligently compiled than first-class records, especially overseas it seems, and, as a result, details of three of the twenty highest limited-overs innings recorded have been impossible to trace - Alan Barrow's 202 not out, Eddie Barlow's 186 and, much to my surprise, Vince Wells' 201. Some of the previous best marks for innings by Surrey batsmen have also proved tricky to uncover. All cases where there is doubt about the previous holder of the record are marked with ***. If anyone can fill in any of the blanks or wishes to tell me about other records set in the match then they can contact me at **tj@sportingdeclarations.co.uk**. We may eventually achieve a full list!

Additionally, in a number of cases a record appears several times in the list below. This is because a new world record is obviously also a new record in the UK and also for the competition and the club concerned. In many of these situations a different 'previous best' was beaten, however, so there is clear value in listing the new mark under each category of record. For example, Ali Brown's individual score beat Graeme Pollock's mark to set the **world** record, Alvin Kallicharran's tally to register the **competition** record, Tom Moody's score to post a new record by a batsman in the **competition against a first-class county** and Grahame Clinton's previous best to secure the Surrey **club** record.

Within each category I have listed records in the following consistent and logical sequence:-
RECORDS FOR - Team Totals; Individual Batting Feats; Partnerships; Match Run Aggregate; Individual Bowling Feats; RECORDS AGAINST - Same order as 'Records For'

WORLD RECORDS

Highest Team Total In Any Limited-Overs Match
Surrey 438-5
beating 413-4 (60 overs) by Somerset v Devon at Torquay in 1990

Highest Team Total By A Side Batting Second In Any Limited-Overs Match
Glamorgan 429
beating 362 by India B v India at Chennai in 2000/01

Highest Individual Score In Any Limited-Overs Match
268 by Alistair Brown
beating 222 not out by Graeme Pollock for Eastern Province v Border at East London in 1974/75

Most Boundaries In An Innings By An Individual In Any Limited-Overs Match
42 (12 sixes and 30 fours) by Alistair Brown
*beating 32(6 sixes and 26 fours) by Graeme Pollock for Eastern Province v Border at East London in 1974/75 ****

Most Double-Centuries Scored By An Individual In First-Class Limited-Overs Cricket
2 by Alistair Brown

Highest Run Aggregate In Any Limited-Overs Match
867 runs (for 15 wkts)
beating 754 (for 16 wkts), India (392-6) v India B (362) at Chennai in 2000/01

Most Expensive Bowling Analysis In Any Limited-Overs Match
9-0-108-3 by Darren Thomas
beating 12-0-107-2 by Chris Lovell for Cornwall v Warwickshire at St. Austell in 1996

UK RECORDS

Highest Team Total In Any Limited-Overs Match In The UK
Surrey 438-5
beating 413-4 (60 overs) by Somerset v Devon at Torquay in 1990

Highest Team Total In Any Limited-Overs Match Between First-Class Counties In The UK
Surrey 438-5
beating 375-4 (40 overs) by Surrey v Yorkshire at Scarborough in the Sunday League in 1994

Highest Team Total By A Side Batting Second Any Limited-Overs Match In The UK
Glamorgan 429
beating 350 (60 overs) by Surrey v Worcestershire at The Oval in 1994

Highest Individual Score In Any Limited-Overs Match In The UK
268 by Alistair Brown
beating 206 by Alvin Kallicharran for Warwickshire v Oxfordshire at Edgbaston in the Nat West Trophy in 1984

Highest Individual Score In Any Limited-Overs Match Between First-Class Counties In The UK
268 by Alistair Brown
beating 203 by Alistair Brown for Surrey v Hampshire at Guildford in the Sunday League in 1997

Most Boundaries In An Innings By An Individual In Any Limited-Overs Match In The UK
42 (12 sixes and 30 fours) by Alistair Brown
beating 31 (11 sixes and 20 fours) by Darren Lehmann for Yorkshire v Nottinghamshire at Scarborough in the National League in 2001 ***

Highest Run Aggregate In Any Limited-Overs Match In The UK
867 runs (for 15 wkts)
beating 707 (for 12 wkts, 60 overs per side) Worcestershire 357-2 v Surrey 350 at the Oval in the Nat West Trophy in 1994

Most Expensive Bowling Analysis In Any Limited-Overs Match In The UK
9-0-108-3 by Darren Thomas
beating 12-0-107-2 by Chris Lovell for Cornwall v Warwickshire at St. Austell in 1996

PREMIER CUP COMPETITION RECORDS

Highest Team Total In The Premier Cup Competition
Surrey 438-5
beating 413-4 (60 overs) by Somerset v Devon at Torquay in 1990

Highest Team Total By A Side Batting Second In The Premier Cup Competition
Glamorgan 429
beating 350 (60 overs) by Surrey v Worcestershire at The Oval in 1994

Highest Individual Score In The Premier Cup Competition
268 by Alistair Brown
beating 206 by Alvin Kallicharran for Warwickshire v Oxfordshire at Edgbaston in 1984

Highest Individual Score Against First-Class Opposition In The Premier Cup Competition
268 by Alistair Brown
beating 180 not out by Tom Moody for Worcestershire v Surrey at The Oval in 1994

Most Boundaries In An Innings By An Individual In The Premier Cup Competition
42 (12 sixes and 30 fours) by Alistair Brown
beating 30 (4 sixes and 26 fours) by Chris Tavare for Somerset v Devon at Torquay in 1990 ***

Highest Run Aggregate In A Match The Premier Cup Competition
867 (for 15 wkts)
beating 707 (for 12 wkts, 60 overs per side) Worcestershire 357-2 v Surrey 350 at The Oval in 1994

Most Expensive Bowling Analysis In The Premier Cup Competition
9-0-108-3 by Darren Thomas
beating 12-0-107-2 by Chris Lovell for Cornwall v Warwickshire at St. Austell in 1996

SURREY CLUB RECORDS

Highest Total By Surrey In All Limited-Overs Competitions
438-5
beating 375-4 (40 overs) v Yorkshire at Scarborough in the Sunday League in 1994

Highest Total By Surrey In The Premier Cup Competition
438-5
beating 350 (60 overs) v Worcestershire at The Oval in 1994

Highest Individual Score By A Surrey Batsman In All Limited-Overs Cricket
268 by Alistair Brown
beating 203 by Alistair Brown v Hampshire at Guildford in the Sunday League in 1997

Highest Individual Score By A Surrey Batsman In The Premier Cup Competition
268 by Alistair Brown
beating 146 by Grahame Clinton v Kent at Canterbury in 1985

Highest Individual Score By A Surrey Batsman Against Glamorgan In All Limited-Overs Cricket
268 by Alistair Brown
beating 119 by Alec Stewart at The Oval in the Sunday League in 1989

Highest Individual Score By A Surrey Batsman Against Glamorgan In The Premier Cup Competition
268 by Alistair Brown
beating 101 not out by David Ward at Swansea in 1992

Most Boundaries In An Innings By A Surrey Batsman In All Limited-Overs Competitions
42 (12 sixes and 30 fours) by Alistair Brown
beating 30 (11 sixes and 19 fours) by Alistair Brown v Hampshire at Guildford in the Sunday League in 1997

Most Boundaries In An Innings By A Surrey Batsman In The Premier Cup Competition
42 (12 sixes and 30 fours) by Alistair Brown
Previous best unknown… possibly 18 (18 fours) by Graham Thorpe v Lancashire at The Oval in 1994

Most Sixes Scored In An Innings By A Surrey Batsman In All Limited-Overs Competitions
12 by Alistair Brown
beating 11 by Alistair Brown v Hampshire at Guildford in the Sunday League in 1997

Most Sixes Scored In An Innings By A Surrey Batsman In The Premier Cup Competition
12 by Alistair Brown
Previous best unknown

Highest Partnership For Any Wicket For Surrey In All Limited-Overs Cricket
286 by Alistair Brown and Ian Ward
beating 218 by Alan Butcher and Geoff Howarth v Gloucestershire at The Oval in the Sunday League in 1976

Highest Partnership For Any Wicket For Surrey In The Premier Cup Competition
286 by Alistair Brown and Ian Ward
beating 180 for the third wicket by Graham Thorpe and David Ward v Lancashire at The Oval in 1994

Highest Opening Partnership For Surrey In All Limited-Overs Cricket
286 by Alistair Brown and Ian Ward
beating 218 by Alan Butcher and Geoff Howarth v Gloucestershire at The Oval in the Sunday League in 1976

Highest Opening Partnership For Surrey In The Premier Cup Competition
286 by Alistair Brown and Ian Ward
beating 164* by Darren Bicknell and Alec Stewart v Dorset at The Oval in 1993

Highest Opening Partnership For Surrey Against Glamorgan In The Premier Cup Competition
286 by Alistair Brown and Ian Ward
beating 57 by John Edrich and Alan Butcher at Cardiff in 1977

Highest Partnership For The Second Wicket For Surrey Against Glamorgan In The Premier Cup Competition
68 by Alistair Brown and Mark Ramprakash
beating
51 by John Edrich and Stewart Storey at The Oval in 1965
and
51 by John Edrich and Geoff Howarth at Cardiff in 1977

Highest Run Aggregate In Any Limited-Overs Match Involving Surrey
867 runs (for 15 wkts)
beating 707 (for 12 wkts, 60 overs per side) Worcestershire 357-2 v Surrey 350 at the Oval in the Nat West Trophy in 1994

Highest Run Aggregate In Any Premier Cup Match Involving Surrey
867 runs (for 15 wkts)
beating 707 (for 12 wkts, 60 overs per side) Worcestershire 357-2 v Surrey 350 at the Oval in 1994

Most Expensive Bowling Analysis By A Surrey Bowler In All Limited-Overs Cricket
10-0-84-2 by Martin Bicknell
beating
*8-0-78-2 by Robin Jackman v Middlesex at The Oval in the Sunday League in 1971 ***
and
*11-0-78-1 by Robin Jackman v Kent at The Oval in the Benson & Hedges Cup in 1973 ***

Most Expensive Bowling Analysis By A Surrey Bowler In The Premier Cup Competition
10-0-84-2 by Martin Bicknell
*beating 10-0-74-1 by Ben Hollioake v Somerset at Taunton in 1999 ***

*** Saqlain Mushtaq's spell of 10-0-82-0 in the Surrey v Glamorgan match, now second on the 'most expensive' list, was completed one over after Bicknell ended his record-breaking stint*

Highest Total Conceded By Surrey In All Limited-Overs Competitions
429
beating 357-2 (60 overs) by Worcestershire at The Oval in the Nat West Trophy in 1994

Highest Total Conceded By Surrey In The Premier Cup Competition
429
beating 357-2(60 overs) by Worcestershire at The Oval in 1994

Most Expensive Bowling Analysis By An Opposition Bowler Against Surrey In All Limited-Overs Competitions
9-0-108-3 by Darren Thomas
beating
10-1-87-3 by Adrian Dalby for Northumberland at Jesmond in the Nat West Trophy in 1989

Most Expensive Bowling Analysis By An Opposition Bowler Against Surrey In The Premier Cup Competition
9-0-108-3 by Darren Thomas
beating
10-1-87-3 by Adrian Dalby for Northumberland at Jesmond in 1989

GLAMORGAN CLUB RECORDS

Highest Total By Glamorgan In All Limited-Overs Competitions
429
beating 373-7 (60 overs) v Bedfordshire at Cardiff in the Nat West Trophy in 1998

Highest Total By Glamorgan In The Premier Cup Competition
429
beating 373-7 (60 overs) v Bedfordshire at Cardiff in 1998

Highest Total By Glamorgan Against A First-Class County In All Limited-Overs Competitions
429
beating 316-8 (60 overs) v Essex at Cardiff in the Nat West Trophy in 1994

Highest Total By Glamorgan Against A First-Class County In The Premier Cup Competition
429
beating 316-8 (60 overs) v Essex at Cardiff in 1994

Highest Total By Glamorgan When Batting Second In All Limited-Overs Competitions
429
beating 314-2 v British Universities at Cambridge in the Benson & Hedges Cup in 1996

Highest Total By Glamorgan When Batting Second In The Premier Cup Competition
429
beating 304-8 (60 overs) v Hampshire at Southampton in 1997

Highest Total By Glamorgan When Batting Second Against A First-Class County In All Limited-Overs Competitions
429
beating 304-8 (60 overs) v Hampshire at Southampton in the Nat West Trophy in 1997

Highest Total By Glamorgan When Batting Second And Losing In Any Limited-Overs Competition
429
beating 299 v Sussex at Hove in the Benson & Hedges Cup in 1998

Highest Total By Glamorgan When Batting Second And Losing In The Premier Cup Competition
429
beating 260 v Somerset at Cardiff in 1978

Fastest Century Scored By A Glamorgan Batsman In All Limited-Overs Competitions
56 balls by Robert Croft
beating 58 balls by Matthew Maynard v British Universities at Cambridge in the Benson & Hedges Cup in 1996

Fastest Century Scored By A Glamorgan Batsman In The Premier Cup Competition
56 balls by Robert Croft
beating 74 balls by Viv Richards v Dorset at Swansea in 1990

Most Boundaries In An Innings By A Glamorgan Batsman In All Limited-Overs Competitions
21 (3 sixes and 18 fours) by Robert Croft
equalling 21 (4 sixes and 17 fours) by Matthew Elliott v Dorset at Bournemouth in the Nat West Trophy in 2000

Most Boundaries In An Innings By A Glamorgan Batsman In The Premier Cup Competition
21 (3 sixes and 18 fours) by Robert Croft
equalling 21 (4 sixes and 17 fours) by Matthew Elliott v Dorset at Bournemouth in 2000

Highest Individual Score By A Glamorgan Batsman Against Surrey In The Premier Cup Competition
119 by Robert Croft
beating 87 by Matthew Maynard at Swansea in 1992

Highest Partnership For The First Wicket For Glamorgan Against Surrey In The Premier Cup Competition
113 by Robert Croft and Ian Thomas
beating 44 by Steve James and Hugh Morris at Swansea in 1992

Highest Partnership For The Fourth Wicket For Glamorgan Against Surrey In The Premier Cup Competition
98 by David Hemp and Adrian Dale
beating 72 by Alan Jones and Alan Rees at Swansea in 1970

Highest Partnership For The Eighth Wicket For Glamorgan Against Surrey In The Premier Cup Competition
65 by Darren Thomas and Michael Kasprowicz
beating 14 by Malcolm Nash and Tony Cordle at Swansea in 1970

Highest Run Aggregate In Any Limited-Overs Match Involving Glamorgan
867 runs (for 15 wkts)
beating 650 (for 11 wkts, 60 overs per side) Glamorgan 345-2 v Durham 305-9 at Darlington in the Nat West Trophy in 1991

Highest Run Aggregate In Any Premier Cup Match Involving Glamorgan
867 runs (for 15 wkts)
beating 650 (for 11 wkts, 60 overs per side) Glamorgan 345-2 v Durham 305-9 at Darlington in 1991

Most Expensive Bowling Analysis By A Glamorgan Bowler In All Limited-Overs Cricket
9-0-108-3 by Darren Thomas
beating 12-1-84-2 by Malcolm Nash v Hampshire at Southampton in the Gillette Cup in 1975

Most Expensive Bowling Analysis By A Glamorgan Bowler In The Premier Cup Competition
9-0-108-3 by Darren Thomas
beating 12-1-84-2 by Malcolm Nash v Hampshire at Southampton in 1975

Glamorgan's Smallest Margin Of Defeat In The Premier Cup Competition
9 runs
beating 10 runs v Warwickshire at Edgbaston in 1972

Highest Total Conceded By Glamorgan In All Limited-Overs Competitions
438-5
beating 371-4 (60 overs) by Hampshire at Southampton in the Gillette Cup in 1975

Highest Total Conceded By Glamorgan In The Premier Cup Competition
438-5
beating 371-4 (60 overs) by Hampshire at Southampton in 1975

Highest Individual Score Conceded By Glamorgan In All Limited-Overs Competitions
268 by Alistair Brown
beating 177 by Gordon Greenidge for Hampshire at Southampton in the Gillette Cup in 1975

Highest Individual Score Conceded By Glamorgan In The Premier Cup Competition
268 by Alistair Brown
beating 177 by Gordon Greenidge for Hampshire at Southampton in 1975

Most Sixes Scored By An Opposition Batsman In An Innings Against Glamorgan In Any Limited-Overs Match
12 by Alistair Brown
beating 8 by Ian Botham for Somerset at Taunton in the Benson And Hedges Cup in 1986

Most Sixes Scored By An Opposition Batsman In An Innings Against Glamorgan In The Premier Cup Competition
12 by Alistair Brown
beating 7 by Gordon Greenidge for Hampshire at Southampton in 1975

Highest Partnership For Any Wicket Conceded By Glamorgan In All Limited-Overs Competitions
286 by Alistair Brown and Ian Ward
beating 223 for the 3rd wicket by Jimmy Cook and Graham Rose for Somerset at Neath in the Sunday League in 1990

Highest Partnership For Any Wicket Conceded By Glamorgan In The Premier Cup Competition
286 by Alistair Brown and Ian Ward
beating 210 for the 1st wicket by Gordon Greenidge and Barry Richards for Hampshire at Southampton in 1975

Highest Opening Partnership Conceded By Glamorgan In All Limited-Overs Competitions
286 by Alistair Brown and Ian Ward
beating 210 by Gordon Greenidge and Barry Richards for Hampshire at Southampton in the Gillette Cup in 1975

Highest Opening Partnership Conceded By Glamorgan In The Premier Cup Competition
286 by Alistair Brown and Ian Ward
beating 210 by Gordon Greenidge and Barry Richards for Hampshire at Southampton in 1975

Most Expensive Bowling Analysis By An Opposition Bowler Against Glamorgan In All Limited-Overs Competitions
10-0-84-2 by Martin Bicknell
beating
10-0-82-0 by John Wood for Durham at Darlington in the Nat West Trophy in 1991
and
10-0-82-2 by Vyvian Pike for Dorset at Bournemouth in the Nat West Trophy in 2000
and
12-0-82-0 by Ian Fantham for Bedfordshire at Cardiff in the Nat West Trophy in 1998

Most Expensive Bowling Analysis By An Opposition Bowler Against Glamorgan In The Premier Cup Competition
10-0-84-2 by Martin Bicknell
beating
10-0-82-0 by John Wood for Durham at Darlington in 1991
and
10-0-82-2 by Vyvian Pike for Dorset at Bournemouth in 2000
and
12-0-82-0 by Ian Fantham for Bedfordshire at Cardiff in 1998

NOTE - Saqlain Mushtaq's spell of 10-0-82-0 in the Surrey v Glamorgan match, now equal second on the 'most expensive' list, was completed one over after Bicknell ended his record-breaking stint

PERSONAL BESTS

ALL LIMITED-OVERS COMPETITIONS

Alistair Brown 268
beating 203 v Hampshire at Guildford in the Sunday League in 1997

Robert Croft 119
beating 114 not out v Middlesex at Cardiff in the National League in 2001

70

Ian Ward 97
beating 91 v Middlesex at Guildford in the Sunday League in 1998

Darren Thomas 71 not out
beating 40 v Hampshire Cricket Board at Southampton in the Nat West Trophy in 1999

PREMIER LIMITED-OVERS CUP COMPETITION

Alistair Brown 268
beating 72 v Holland at the Oval in 1996

Robert Croft 119
beating 64 v Bedfordshire at Cardiff in 1997

Ian Ward 97
beating 81 v Yorkshire at Headingley in 2001

Darren Thomas 71 not out
beating 40 v Hampshire Cricket Board at Southampton in 1999

Michael Kasprowicz 25
beating 15 for Leicestershire v Ireland at Clontarf, Dublin in 1999

Ian Thomas 23
beating 11 v Somerset at Taunton in 2001

Adam Hollioake 5-77
beating 4-53 v Middlesex at the Oval in 1995

ACKNOWLEDGEMENTS

First and foremost my thanks go to Ali Brown, and the supporting cast in an incredible match, without whom this book would not have been possible! Thanks to Ali for a full and frank interview and to all those Surrey players who answered my questions about the match. Grateful thanks also to those listed below who helped me with photos and statistical data.

PHOTOGRAPHS
Peter Frost
Phil Walter and Adam Davey of Empics
Joan Elgar

STATISTICAL ASSISTANCE
Richard Arnold (Surrey statistics)
Dr Andrew Hignell (corroboration of Glamorgan statistics)
Philip Bailey (cricinfo)

RUN CHART
Mark Smith

OTHER
Sue Leach (proofreading)
Johnny Grave and Jeff Hancock, Surrey CCC
Don Scott and Ray Kasey, Cheam CC

Other Books By Trevor Jones

The following books by Trevor Jones about Surrey County Cricket Club are still available and may be purchased directly from the publisher at the discounted prices detailed below.

Order from **Sporting Declarations Books, Dept AB, P.O. Box 882, SUTTON, SM2 5AW.**
Cheques/postal orders payable to *Sporting Declarations Books*, please.

Pursuing The Dream - My Season With Surrey C.C.C.

The ultimately doomed Championship challenge of 1998 forms the central plank of Trevor Jones' first book, a fan's diary of a season following his team around the country. The author's personal day-by-day account of the summer balances sharp observations and opinions on both the county and international game with tales of the lighter moments of his season with Surrey. Received impressive critical acclaim, including a three-ball review in Wisden Cricket Monthly.

Published April 1999
256 pages
Hardback edition 0 9535307 0 1   Price - £8.99 (inc UK p&p)
Softback edition 0 9535307 1 X   Price - £4.99 (inc UK p&p)

The Dream Fulfilled - Surrey's 1999 County Championship Triumph

The most detailed account of a Championship-winning season ever written, *'The Dream Fulfilled'* records Surrey's first County Championship triumph for twenty-eight years. Features full descriptions of every session of play, along with exclusive in-depth interviews with the players, twenty-four pages of full-colour photos, run charts and official Surrey CCC scorebook extracts of significant innings/events, press quotes and views from the other counties. Highly acclaimed everywhere it was reviewed, this book will be treasured by Surrey fans for years to come.

Published April 2000
376 pages, including 24 pages of full-colour photographs
Hardback only   0 9535307 2 8   Price - £13.99 (inc UK p&p)

Doubling Up With Delight - Surrey's Twin Triumphs 2000

The in-depth story of Surrey's first-ever double-winning season when they added the National League Division Two title to a second successive County Championship victory. The author's presence at every day's play ensures that each session is again covered in detail and embellished with fascinating dressing room insights from the players. Run charts, scorebook extracts and twenty-four pages of colour photos are again included in another essential volume for followers of Surrey County Cricket Club.

Published April 2001
312 pages, including 24 pages of full-colour photographs
Softback only   0 9535307 3 6   Price - £12.99 (inc UK p&p)

Further information and a special multiple-purchase book deal can be found at
www.sportingdeclarations.co.uk

Comments can be directed to the author at **tj@sportingdeclarations.co.uk**

72